DUTY OF CARE

DUTY OF CARE

An Executive's Guide for Corporate Boards in the Digital Era

ALIZABETH CALDER

WILEY

Published by John Wiley & Sons, Inc., Hoboken, New Jersey.
Published simultaneously in Canada.

For general information on our other products and services or for technical support, please contact our Customer Care Department within the United States at (800) 762-2974, outside the United States at (317) 572-3993, or fax (317) 572-4002.

Wiley publishes in a variety of print and electronic formats and by print-on-demand. Some material included with standard print versions of this book may not be included in e-books or in print-on-demand. If this book refers to media such as a CD or DVD that is not included in the version you purchased, you may download this material at http://booksupport.wiley.com. For more information about Wiley products, visit www.wiley.com.

Library of Congress Cataloging-in-Publication Data

Names: Calder, Alizabeth, 1958- author.
Title: Duty of care : an executive's guide for corporate boards in the digital era / Alizabeth Calder.
Description: Hoboken, New Jersey : John Wiley & Sons, Inc., [2019] | Includes bibliographical references and index. |
Identifiers: LCCN 2019006656 (print) | LCCN 2019009174 (ebook) | ISBN 9781119578130 (ePDF) | ISBN 9781119578192 (ePub) | ISBN 9781119578154 (hardback)
Subjects: LCSH: Boards of directors. | Corporate governance. | Information technology—Management.
Classification: LCC HD2745 (ebook) | LCC HD2745 .C35 2019 (print) | DDC 658.4/22—dc23
LC record available at https://lccn.loc.gov/2019006656

Cover Design: Wiley
Cover Image: © Alexander Supertramp/Shutterstock

Printed in the United States of America

V10009034_032519

Dedicated with gratitude to Tom, Geoff, and Avery for their support and encouragement.

Dedicated with appreciation for my readers and supporters. Vic, Celia, Leonie, and Mike, thank you.

Dedicated with respect to all corporate leaders who understand the impact of technology on all of their stakeholders and incorporate that understanding in operations, oversight, and strategy.

CONTENTS

INTRODUCTION

In the lead up to the banking crisis of 2008, smart PhDs developed complex formulas that aggregated large volumes of high-risk mortgages and made it seem as if those funds were the next great investment opportunity. They even created a whole new vocabulary, using terms like *synthetic derivatives* to sound even more clever, while they effectively hid the risks of the subprime mortgage market.

The magnitude of the collapse suggests that many directors were taken in. They must not have really understood what was being done, or they would never have agreed. They ignored the terms they did not understand and trusted the smart people to have fully thought through the strategic and risk implications.

It is human nature to behave as if we understand things when we do not. Responsible boards need to ask more questions to make sure that they understand.

Technology is the next vulnerable frontier. The new mantra for corporate directors needs to be *if you cannot explain it so I can understand it, I will not support what you are proposing. You need to explain it so I can understand it. Duty of Care* is designed to help.

Case Studies!

Duty of Care gives you case studies ... specific examples where a board either really messed up, or they really got it right, with a very clear takeaway from each example:

What the companies that messed up can teach us:

Yahoo – Boards who ignore cyber-related issues do so at their (share price) peril.

Equifax – Boards need to demonstrate oversight of cybersecurity.

Home Depot – Lack of understanding or knowledge is no longer a defense.

Loblaw – The governance of large technology investments takes as much attention and oversight as investments in M&A or corporate expansion.

Volkswagen – Boards need to enable ease of access for whistleblowers in all aspects of the business.

Wells Fargo – Boards need to know that problems are really understood.

Fortunately, we can also learn from examples of companies really getting it right:

Burberry – Board leadership includes understanding how new technologies can enhance value.

Compass Group PLC – Board competence includes using technology to solve business problems.

BlackBerry – The board really understanding what its business differentiators are can breathe new life into a struggling company.

Visa – Boards can deliver exponential value by looking at sector-level trends to find ways to reposition.

Amazon – Boards need to stay focused on where the facts take them. Just because there is technology involved does not mean that they can lose sight of the basics.

Smart Questions!

Duty of Care also gives you Smart Questions organized by the topics you need to understand. They will help you know what things you should be thinking about, and frame your conversations with the smart-but-maybe-terrifying people who may confuse you. This book will equip you to lead your board conversations by helping you lead management to understand what you, as the board, need to know.

Fulsome Explanations, in Case You Need More Information!

Finally, *Duty of Care* offers a fulsome but easy-to-understand discussion on most of the topics that you may find yourself considering. You can start with the Case Studies and Smart Questions. Then, use the written material to help interpret the answers and broaden your own foundations to genuinely understand the risks and productively discuss the opportunities that technology can offer.

In September 2016, the once dominant Internet giant Yahoo, while in negotiations to sell itself to Verizon, announced that in 2014 it had been the victim of a data breach. The attack compromised the names and contact information of 500 million users. It was the biggest data breach in history.

Three months later, Yahoo further disclosed that a breach in 2013 had also compromised one billion accounts. In addition to names and contact information, customer security questions and answers were also compromised.

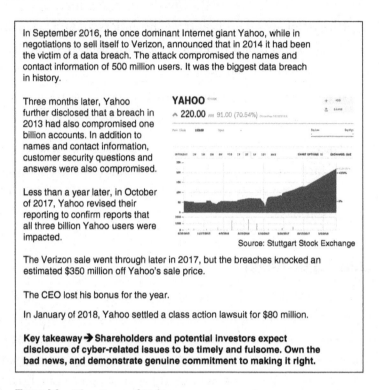

YAHOO
220.00
91.00 (70.54%)
Source: Stuttgart Stock Exchange

Less than a year later, in October of 2017, Yahoo revised their reporting to confirm reports that all three billion Yahoo users were impacted.

The Verizon sale went through later in 2017, but the breaches knocked an estimated $350 million off Yahoo's sale price.

The CEO lost his bonus for the year.

In January of 2018, Yahoo settled a class action lawsuit for $80 million.

Key takeaway➔Shareholders and potential investors expect disclosure of cyber-related issues to be timely and fulsome. Own the bad news, and demonstrate genuine commitment to making it right.

Figure I.1 The Case of Yahoo

Let's start with the case of Yahoo, shown in Figure I.1.

What questions did the board ask of Yahoo management before the breach was fully disclosed? If the directors were asking questions, did they understand the answers, or did they rely on other people to interpret?

- Directors do not simply ask the accountant if the numbers are correct. They learn how to read auditor's notes.
- Directors would never approve a transaction without asking questions about the deal's scope, terms, and risks. They would ask questions about industry, regulations and the other things they need to know.

But when it comes to technology decisions, many directors rely on the staff to understand the risks and to know what to invest in. Whether through fear or ignorance, most corporate directors are not providing effective governance.

Duty of Care covers everything you need to be effective and self-sufficient.

Chapter 1 – Basics and Essentials

The book starts with an overview of the types of technology, in accessible language, so you can hold your own in conversations. As with understanding what earnings before interest, tax, depreciation, and amortization (EBITDA) is to talk about earnings, you need a basic vocabulary.

You will have a framework to understand the essentials – social, mobile, data and cloud – so you can confidently engage in both risk and strategy conversations. In addition, *Duty of Care* de-mystifies emerging technologies, like block chain and AI, so you are fully empowered as an active and informed director.

Chapters 2 through 5 – Risk and Cybersecurity

Cybersecurity and cyber-risk are among the most stress-inducing topics faced by directors, for good reason:

- 57% of companies don't believe that they would detect a sophisticated cyber attack.
- 61% of organizations say they have had a recent cybersecurity incident.

- 98% of organizations don't believe that their cybersecurity function is up to the job.

Chapters 2 through 5 consider four predominant aspects of cyber-risk:

Chapter 2 – Risk: What really matters as you endeavor to protect the company's interests while balancing the need to verify your controls posture as part of your duty-of-care obligation?

Chapter 3 – Cybersecurity: How do you deal with your specific responsibilities for the ever-changing demands of cyber security?

Chapter 4 – Enterprise Risk Management: How do you effectively address more general risk issues as part of an overarching oversight program?

Chapter 5 – Digitally Driven Litigation and Fraud: How do you think about the emerging issues, particularly board-level exposures, which now include securities fraud?

Duty of Care arms you with director-appropriate insight into the actual risks and the regulatory requirements, including strategies for meaningful and effective oversight.

Chapters 6 through 8 – Technology Strategy and Investment

Since 2000, 52% of the companies in the Fortune 500 have gone bankrupt, been acquired, or have ceased to exist, due in large part to the disruption of traditional industry models . . . and yet . . .

> Only 35% of companies say they are investing in digital as part of their overall strategy.[1]

Navigating how much to invest, what to invest in, and how to prioritize your investments is a bit like being in a "perfect storm," as shown in Figure I.2.

Each of the weather patterns has its own momentum. Each is daunting. The eye of the storm is where things are most clear.

Consider the example of Microsoft. In 2016, they seemed to be losing their advantage as the more ubiquitous platform of Apple took dominance. The CEO and board decided that finding a new customer base or market segment was a strategic imperative. They found clarity in accessibility technology. For Microsoft, the eye of the storm offered unmet and even unanticipated needs in the market that they could uniquely satisfy. In a very short time, Microsoft became a world leader in delivering solutions for people with disabilities.

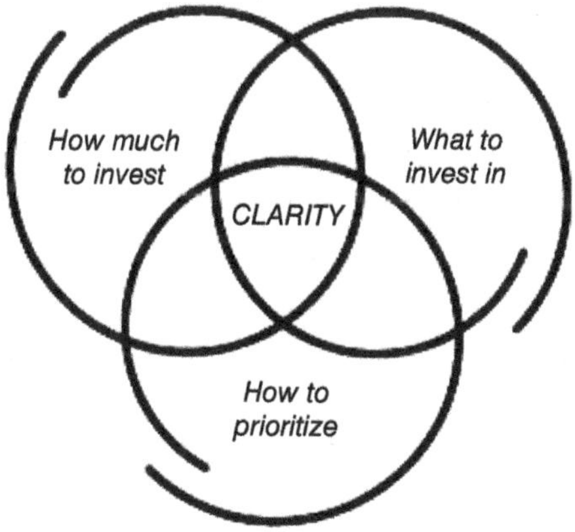
How much to invest
What to invest in
CLARITY
How to prioritize

Figure I.2 The Perfect Storm

Chapter 6 – Start with how much to invest. How much to invest depends on what technology you have already, and how proactive you want to be. Do you want to be a leader or a follower? Understanding your company's maturity will help you assess how much investment is right for you, and how aggressively you can expect to progress.

Not every company has to be the digital leader, but intent and leadership are key. Companies with a higher level of digital maturity are 9% to 26% more profitable than their average industry competitors,[2] so you need to be deliberate and understand the risks if you are investing as a follower. Drawing on your newly developed vocabulary, ask questions about what investments are being made. Make sure that investment plans align with your business strategy.

Top-decile companies track their IT spending to have no more than 75% of it going to steady state. Does your management team look at how their spending is aligned? What should you be investing the strategic 25% on?

Chapter 7 – Think about what your company's priority should be. This chapter gives you an example of how to consider new opportunities. Traditional business models, like Porter's Five Forces,[3] can help you set priorities:

- What attracts investors and customers in the digital age?
- How can suppliers add accretive value?
- Where your assumptions about your competition could be out-dated.

What do you need to accomplish to hold (or improve) your position?

Chapter 8 – Find Clarity. Think of clarity as confidence. You should feel ready to articulate your technology vision and sense of direction as part of a genuine conversation with your CEO and other board members.

Today's competent director can articulate what an investor would want to know about the company's technology strategy. Directors demonstrate important leadership and they can comprehend the elevator version of the company's digital aspirations.

The chapter is focused on the best-practice leadership concepts that uniquely resonate in the technology aspects of investment oversight. It provides the smart questions to help you find clarity.

Chapter 9 – Oversight

In 2017, Hurricane Irma was so far off the expected landfall that cities like Naples, Florida, took the brunt of the damage because they didn't know they needed to prepare, whereas on the east coast of the state the cities were prepared beyond what they needed. Winds shift, and weather patterns are unpredictable.

Technology governance is like managing in that perfect storm, so you need to understand the external factors to know where the eye of the storm is actually going to touch down. See Figure I.3.

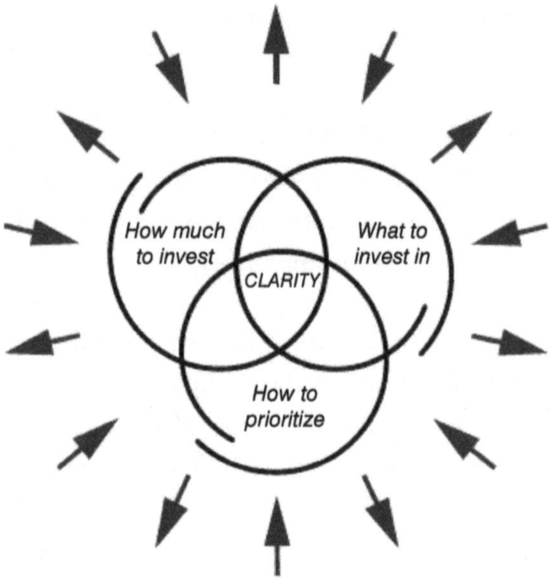
How much
to invest
What to
invest in
CLARITY
How to
prioritize

Figure I.3 The External Factors

On the positive side, the winds that push and pull can make technology governance a unique opportunity. It is one of the few areas in which you can directly influence the outcome of your investment. It is as if you can buy a stock, and then be in the boardroom making the decisions that will affect share price.

On the negative side, those winds are also multipliers for risk. Every miscalculation can be magnified through speed and volume.

Governance experts are converging on the view that "it is insufficient for the board to say that they delegated responsibility to the CEO when major strategic investments fail."[4] It is strategically important that the board have:

Measurable indicators of progress.

Defined outcomes.

Regular monitoring of results.

Anything less is a failure.[5] For purposes of your digital strategy and technology investment, *Duty of Care* considers navigating those prevailing winds as functions of oversight.

Chapter 10 – Governance

The final chapter of the book takes it up a level to the broader considerations aligned with your duty of care:

- The need to "enhance and protect" value.
- Continuous improvement of your own competence.
- Smart Questions considering both investment and risk.

* * *

Today's director does not have to settle for confusing risk updates or opaque investment proposals. It should be the exception rather than the rule that you need outside help to know the right questions to ask. You should not have to agree to an investment and then wait a year and hope that it all works out as expected.

Use the targeted Smart Questions at the end of each chapter to genuinely understand where you have risk and where you have opportunity.

Duty of Care will help you develop your strategy, so you can weather the storm.

Notes

1. "Only 43% of Canadian Companies Could Detect a Sophisticated Cyber-attack," *EY Newsroom* (February 15, 2017).
2. Westerman, G., Bonnet, D., and McAfee, A., "The Advantages of Digital Maturity," *MIT Sloan Management Review* (November 20, 2012).
3. Porter, M. "What Is Strategy?" *Harvard Business Review* (November–December 1996).
4. "Why Single Out Technology Governance for Board Attention?" *Enterprise Governance Blog* (February 16, 2014).
5. Ibid.

Chapter 1

Basics and Essentials

In 2006, classic brand Burberry was facing a diminishing market position and a significant operating margin challenge. It almost disappeared from the market. Ten years later, the brand is back at the top as a luxury brand, thanks in large part to a board and CEO taking the time to learn the language and invest in technology.

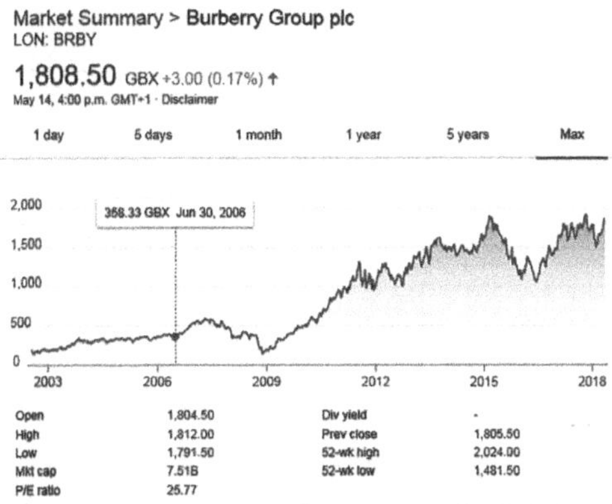

Market Summary > Burberry Group plc
LON: BRBY
1,808.50 GBX +3.00 (0.17%) ↑
May 14, 4:00 p.m. GMT+1 · Disclaimer
1 day
5 days
1 month
1 year
5 years
Max
2,000
1,500
1,000
500
0
358.33 GBX Jun 30, 2006
2003
2006
2009
2012
2015
2018
Open 1,804.50
High 1,812.00
Low 1,791.50
Mkt cap 7.51B
P/E ratio 25.77
Div yield -
Prev close 1,805.50
52-wk high 2,024.00
52-wk low 1,481.50

Source: London Stock Exchange

Burberry moved its full brand experience into a social and mobile presence. That decision delivered unparalleled access to retail-enthusiastic millennials. Strategies included the Art of the Trench social networking site in 2009, providing a compelling lifestyle engagement. In 2012, the brand ran a prelaunch on their 2012 trench coat line in a "buy now" program tied to Instagram and Twitter. Continuing to innovate, stores were equipped with live-streaming tied to RFID sensors in the store so if a customer picks up an item a related video will run on a nearby screen.

Burberry is now partnering with innovators like WeChat to deliver an immersive experience in their retail stores. The result has been a gross margin increase from 59% to 76%, economic profit growth from $92 million to $435 million, and a total shareholder return (CAGR) of 17% over 10 years. The share price says it all.

The case of Burberry takeaway ➔ Expect your business strategy team to bring you insight and help you understand how new technologies could solve business problems.

Figure 1.1 The Case of Burberry

Burberry's transformation did not start with the CIO (see Figure 1.1). It started with the CEO and the board asking questions. This chapter will give you the vocabulary to ask the questions and understand the answers.

A couple of qualifiers:

1. Not everything discussed will be relevant for you, but you should understand all the concepts. If you don't know that a technology exists and what it can do, how will you know when to consider it?
2. Many technologists thrive on being opaque. They use overly complicated words. Do not let unfamiliar words stop you from understanding.
3. Your IT leaders are setting strategy with the tactical decisions they make every day. Your company may have to live with those decisions for a long time, and they may dramatically limit the options that you have. You need to set the direction, so the tactical decisions are aligned and enabling.

A capable director does not need an in-depth understanding of every new technology or trend. In fact, the pace of change makes it impossible for even technology leaders to stay abreast of every new concept. You can achieve an appropriate working knowledge by understanding four key dynamics that influence technology, and by periodically recalibrating your view of the implications for your business.

A simple model shows the core dimensions to basically understand, as shown in Figure 1.2.

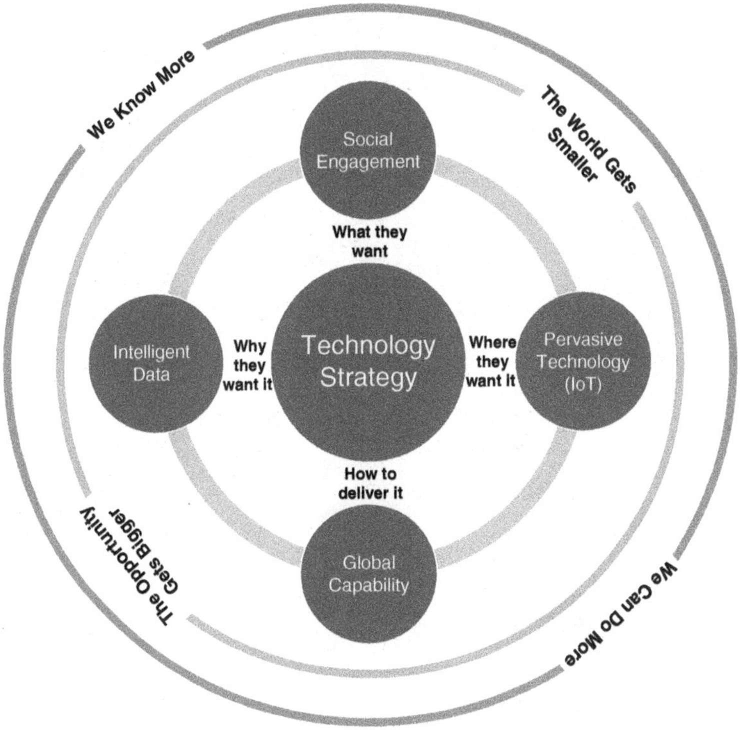
We Know More
The World Gets Smaller
We Can Do More
The Opportunity Gets Bigger
Social Engagement
What they want
Intelligent Data
Why they want it
Technology Strategy
Where they want it
Pervasive Technology (IoT)
How to deliver it
Global Capability

Figure 1.2 Core Dynamics of a Technology Strategy

Consider how the model supported Burberry, as shown in Figure 1.3.

First, they engaged the customers on their mobile devices, at the top right quadrant of the model (between Social Media and Pervasive Technology). They used ad campaigns and in-store promotions to encourage Burberry as a place and a brand to talk about. Tools like Facebook let them see what was resonating with their customers – that is, what was trending – so they could stay closely aligned and drive the right messages and promotions to the right customers in the right way at the right time. Social media and pervasive

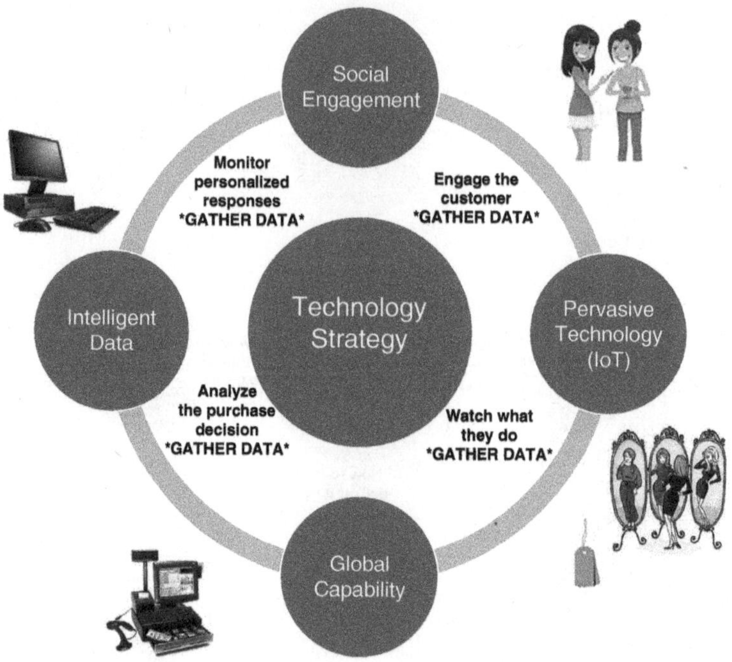
Social Engagement
Monitor personalized responses *GATHER DATA*
Engage the customer *GATHER DATA*
Intelligent Data
Technology Strategy
Pervasive Technology (IoT)
Analyze the purchase decision *GATHER DATA*
Watch what they do *GATHER DATA*
Global Capability

Figure 1.3 The Example of Burberry's Strategy

devices let them see where customers were and what they were shopping for.

In addition to letting Burberry collect individual information about each customer, social media let them aggregate information from the customer's extended social network; if one customer's tweet or Snapchat photo caused people in their social network to look at more Burberry information, they knew they had a successful product or campaign.

Burberry also dialed up their data gathering by using pervasive devices like sensors in mirrors and product tags.

Those sensors could recognize the customer by their mobile device and co-relate their interests and behaviors based on where in the store they were most engaged – what displays caused them to stop, and where in the store they tried things on. They were able to engage in real-time direct marketing, including offering immediately relevant messages to the customer's mobile device with in-store offers.

Continuing around the bottom of the model, delivery capabilities like cloud made it possible to aggregate data globally and tie together behavior at point-of-sale and online. Global capability let them bring together all aspects of the customer's activity, including purchase decisions.

Continuing around to the top of the model, Burberry leveraged deep data analytics to inform "artificial" intelligence (AI), enabling computer systems capable of understanding the customer's behavior to make relevant offers.

Each step that Burberry took around the model gave them more intelligent data, which was at the center of their technology strategy. Gathering data at each step around the model let Burberry move the customer closer to both purchase and loyalty.

The pages that follow break down each of the four core dynamics to help you think your way around the model and find ideas that will add value. Use the model to have satisfying conversations with your CIO, your CEO, and the rest of the board.

(Note: Definitions for jargon and acronyms are also summarized in a table at the back of the book, for reference later.)

Social Engagement

At the top of the core dynamics model is *social engagement.* Not that long ago, the focus was simply on the power of social media to have people pay attention to your company. The leverage came from having your marketing team work to keep the attention positive. Today, social media has become a powerful source of engagement that can directly work to grow your business and measure your effectiveness.

Social Media ROI – Social media contributors can be measured and provide insight in four areas[1]:

1. Consumption – You should know how many people view or download your content.
2. Sharing – You should know if the content you are putting out there is gaining momentum.
3. Lead Generation – You should know exactly how your content is generating leads, or creating real interest in making a purchase.
4. Conversion to Sales – You should know what specific content drives sales, and you should be measuring the monetary value of those sales.

With the right measurements in place, your board should see a direct relationship between social media and ROI.

Social Media Leverage – The new power of social media is realized when you become part of the user's lifestyle. That leverage comes from new technologies like wearable devices, sensors, gamification, and personalization. Consider some examples:

- **Fitbit** is an example of a wearable device that helps people improve their health and lifestyle by using sensors to track and report on activity levels.
- Users of Fitbit also use the Fitbit app. They can invite their fit-focused friends to join a group, making their fitness activity a shared lifestyle. By encouraging fitness enthusiasts to challenge each other through the app, Fitbit created a game that could be shared by socially connected communities. That use of gamelike features to improve engagement is called gamification.
- **Bing, Yelp, and Yahoo** are examples of companies transforming their business model using geo-fencing, which is the creation of a virtual perimeter that represents a real-world geographic area. When you are online, and your computer asks if it can identify your current location, the site you are using is applying geo-fencing to be more relevant for you. On a mobile device, apps dynamically make shopping and dining recommendations that are specific to exactly where you are at the time.
- Retailer Urban Outfitters saw a 75% increase in sales by tracking customer devices in the store and then sending offers tied directly to the section of the store that the customer was in.[2]

- Our earlier **Burberry** example took social media engagement to new heights by talking to customers real-time and getting those customers to share their shopping with social media friends. Engagement worked – customers bought more.
- ***International airports*** are leveraging the most powerful strategic "social" tool so far – personalization. By knowing that the app user is in the airport, and offering faster check-in or automated customs processing, airports now provide offers that are uniquely relevant to the person, the place, and the time. This self-focused trend is also known as the Internet-of-Me.

Digital marketing experts believe that these combined social-media experiences are becoming more important than either price or product[3]:

- By 2018 over 50% of companies will redirect investments toward customer experience innovation. Source: Gartner
- Eighty-one percent of consumers want brands to understand them better and know when and when not to approach them. Source: Accenture
- Sixty percent of marketers struggle to personalize content in real time, yet 77% believe real-time personalization is crucial. Source: Adobe

Social Media Risk – There is an important paradox developing around social media. On one side, consumers want their experience to be hyperpersonalized, and they want their brands to know them well and engage accordingly. On the other side, there is increasing scrutiny on how information about a social user's behavior is being used. The point of inflection came when Facebook was found to be selling behavioral analytics for its 87 million users. Until then, most social users seemed to be unaware or unconcerned about their right to privacy.

Facebook's sale of users' personal and behavioral data will drive fundamental changes for many business models. Regulatory requirements for transparency and consent will have a dramatic impact. As a director, you need to be prepared to discuss the risks. The Smart Questions later in this chapter are designed to help you balance the opportunities and the emerging issues in social media.

The final consideration in social media is your company's own presence. Even if you are not actively using social media, your Corporate Relations work should include knowing (and managing) what is being said about your company, your executives and your fellow directors. For reference, Figure 1.4 offers some extra notes on *responding to issues with your social media presence*.

A final note on social media – If you think social media is important for your company, you'll want to also understand analytics and artificial intelligence. More about those concepts follow.

Many governance conversations focus on how to respond when social media conversations tend toward the negative. Traditional crisis management disciplines apply:

First, you have to know that it is happening, in real time. Even if social media isn't high on your radar, by definition social media isn't about you—it's about the influencers and opinions that are outside your control. You need to be investing at least enough to have timely warning.

Second, your organization needs to have enough information to know if the situation warrants a response or if it can be expected to blow over and is better left without comment. Given the viral nature of social media, risk factors scale quickly in a bad situation, time is not your friend. This requires investment in intelligence about who is saying what, where, and how. This doesn't mean a herd of geeks, trolling social media for conversations. There are lots of tools available to monitor social media, and flag potential threats for analysis and response planning—use one.

Third, think about the actual message you are conveying. Almost as important as having a crisis communication plan is owning your mistakes. In the Facebook data breach early in 2018, Zuckerberg made the situation much worse by taking the better part of a week to apologize and own the situation (even then, he was the target of criticism for referring to "what happened" instead of "what we let happen"). If you are using social media, you need to be prepared to own it.

Finally, look at who is formulating your social media response plan. Your social strategy, and particularly incident responses, need to closely parallel your corporate presence. Don't let your organization default this task to a socially savvy but relatively inexperienced spokesperson. The person actually crafting the message is driving your social strategy by default.

- Have clear business policies and rules for all social engagement.
- Look to more prudent, mature employees to manage this critical part of your corporate massaging.

In *Making Sense of Social Media*, industry expert Erik Linask observes "Social is easier to teach than corporate responsibility". SOURCE: Linask, E. *Making Sense of Social Media*, Techzone 360 (January 30, 2012).

Figure 1.4 Responding to Issues with Your Social Media Presence

Pervasive Technology (IoT)

Pervasive technology has extended well beyond the original notion of portable devices like a laptop computer, tablet, or cell phone. Ubiquity of connectivity combined with highly capable micro devices has created opportunity for new and unique mobile tools. Technology like smart cars and smart appliances are affording the Internet unlimited capacity to connect people, places, and things. Digital connections seem to be limited only by imagination and investment capital. As size and interoperability of devices evolves, a new dimension has developed known as the Internet of Things (IoT).

As soon as someone hits 'Send' the information or images are out there and can never really be taken back. A store can gather information about your buying behavior and preferences by tracking your movement when you are shopping. A pair of glasses can disguise a video recording device.

IoT is a great opportunity for engagement and sales, but it is also a risk for consent and privacy. The three steps that follow will let you engage with confidence in related conversations.

First, consider the possibilities – Think about how mobile devices are being used:

- A phone can connect with a car.
- Home monitoring systems can keep you connected, including taking an action like locking a door or seeing who is ringing the doorbell from your phone.

- A refrigerator can tell you what groceries you need.
- A car can be connected to traffic monitoring, including sensors that tell the car to brake if they identify an obstacle.
- Car navigation systems, using GPS, can help drivers both find a destination and avoid traffic.
- Handheld devices have industrial applications. For example, railyard teams can use them to know exactly where the moving stock is; entertainment venue staff can validate legitimate tickets at point of entry; farmers can place sensors in the field to test for moisture and trigger watering systems

No device, product, or industry is unaffected. Mobile is not your grandma's car phone anymore.

Next, explore and appreciate the trends – Where there were previously significant barriers to adoption, mobile technologies are now ubiquitous:

- The most recent (2018) estimates are that 95% of Americans have at least one cell phone.[4]
- Barcode scanners that talk to mobile devices let even the smallest of companies manage inventory, offer promotions, and verify an unlimited number of attributes instantly.
- Sensors that track and transmit real-time information are revolutionizing quality control and safety in industries like produce and frozen food shipment.

- Pattern recognition is being applied to practical solutions like offering consumers the ability to take a photo of a product on their mobile device and then directly scan the Internet for similar products and competitive pricing.

As technology becomes user-friendly, accurate and affordable, there is an opportunity, but there is also a risk. Consider BlackBerry's early decision to ignore the need for mobile apps. They made an investment decision to maintain a closed architecture, meaning that they made it difficult for other companies to create apps for their devices. Unfortunately, that decision meant that it was easier, faster, and cheaper to develop apps for the iPhone, so the iPhone took the largest share of the app-driven market. BlackBerry lost market share because they decided to block what became a core set of capabilities.

Finally, embrace mobile as a service not a solution – A successful mobile strategy delivers a service or a feature. For example, Audi has now turned cars into just another mobile device by letting customers identify their car on a shared cell phone plan. Users no longer need to connect their phone to their car to have access to their cell phone service – the car has that power all by itself.

In addition, mobile services are no longer specific to the device they are on. Once a service has been developed, if it is on new technology it can be moved to other devices with relative ease. A mobile offering may be a foundational investment, preparing you for more broadly based products in the future. The mobile device itself is not the differentiator any more. What will differentiate your business is how, when, and where the device would be used. Focus on the outcome, rather than the device or service.

For example, imagine if a grocery chain offered you a grocery-list app that let you keep your list in your phone and, when you arrived at any of their stores, it guided you through the most direct route to get in and out with the things you need. Busy customers using the app will quickly develop a preference for that specific chain. Think through a day in the life of your target customer, and you can begin to imagine the places and services that might be useful.

A note on large industrial uses of pervasive technology – Discussions of mobile technology tend toward consumer examples, because they are relatable for everyone. Mobile technology also has important nonconsumer applications. For example, mobile is also being used to enable workflow improvements in compliance-heavy sectors like railroads and oil fields. By using a radio frequency identifier (RFID) to monitor inspections, railroads can deliver tracking in the yard, which eliminates the need for paper-based tracking and end-of-shift reporting.

Imagine if the trains that derailed in the Lac-Mégantic rail disaster had been equipped with sensors that would verify brake systems were engaged. A warning signal could have been sent to the engineer to tell them that they were too far from the train without the safety mechanisms in place. Crisis averted.

Investment in mobile technology lets you differentiate your product in ways that customers will value. Consider National car rental's any-car-in-the-aisle strategy. It lets customers just walk up to a car and drive away. We don't have to know exactly how National has made this service possible to imagine the possibilities. We can guess that National knows the customer has arrived, so maybe RFID talking to the customer's phone is involved. National also knows, without a person being involved, which car the customer chose. That could be enabled by near field communications (NFC), where two devices communicate independently when they recognize each other in a defined proximity.

That is all it takes, and the customer is good to drive away.

Keep thinking about the possibilities. Attendants can be eliminated by using sensors to match the customer's mobile device and the reservation. The next thing National could offer is a "coffee please" setting on a reservation. The Starbucks app would know their preferred beverage, and the customer can pick up their order on their way out. There really are no limits anymore.

Even if we do not know exactly how National is enabling their service, just by thinking about how they might be doing it lets us study what is unique or compelling. Get curious:

- If you see someone doing something interesting with their phone, ask about it.
- If you see a new consumer service being offered, think about how they are doing it.

- If you see something interesting, a quick search on Google will give you some surprising insight.
- Brainstorm "day in the life of" your customer or partner with your CEO and CIO.
- Ask your CIO what opportunities they think might exist for your mobile strategy.

Mobile is all around you, and almost every sector is pushing the limits. You need to know at least enough to keep up.

I once asked a 10-year-old how to do something on my brand-new-latest-and-greatest iPhone (I was a BlackBerry die-hard). Right after he showed me how to do what I wanted, he told his father that the phone I had was wasted on me.

Don't be offended; just keep asking questions until you understand what you were curious about.

Global Capability

Global capability, the most recognized example being Cloud, speaks to utility-based services. Instead of building computer capability with hardware, software, and operating system, a company can buy a service that provides all the required foundations and is managed to specified service levels. In a non-Cloud world, data is stored in a defined location where access and integration require investment to bring disparate data sources together. With a Cloud data solution, data can be accessible across broadly based locations and extended real time for analysis and operational effectiveness.

If we consider it as an example, Cloud can apply to processing capacity, memory capacity or solutions (like software) purchased as a service. The advent of Cloud represents an investment inflection point, by making it easy to adopt new technology without tying up either investment capital or time. It may let you tap a wealth of capability at a fraction of the cost. It may also level the playing field by providing mature and complex capabilities on demand—start-ups no longer need the lead time or capital to compete with established companies. With pervasive, cheap access, a company of any size can weave capability maturity, operational excellence, and compliance disciplines into their business value proposition.

Cloud computing is becoming the default way to manage technology, and includes:

- Managed business services like Microsoft Office, for email and spreadsheets.
- Specific software requirements, provided as a service (SaaS), to support business functions like financial accounting and human resources.
- Integrated enterprise resource planning (ERP) business solutions like SAP, and Oracle.

Only the most unique businesses now need to develop or customize software to meet the needs of the business. There are many advantages to buying a service instead:

- **Currency** – SaaS providers maintain the most current software versions, so you have seamless access to the newest and best capabilities.

- **Discipline** – Sound operational and compliance disciplines ensure that important software updates are current.
- **Measurements and reporting** – SaaS providers follow standard processes, known as use cases, aligning the specific requirements with defined and measurable business outcomes.
- **Flexibility** – Cloud cost models are consumption-based, so you can ramp up, or down, as required.
- **Integration** – Where solutions have multiple components, such as the CRM that is part of the ERP system, software will be integrated, managed and maintained by the service provider, reducing the risks associated with change management and interface maintenance.
- **Application programming interfaces** – Rather than having unique interfaces to maintain, SaaS providers use application programming interfaces (APIs) to standardize how systems talk to each other.

More about integrations and APIs – There is a significant cost and risk in making systems talk to each other. Even if it is built correctly, an interface must be tested any time there is a change in either system. APIs use standard protocols and structured building blocks, so interfaces are easier to manage and more reliable.

An analogy would be crossing a stream. Before APIs, a developer had to continually assess all the rocks in the stream and map a path to safely get from one shore to the other. In addition, as water levels changed, or the people crossing were more (or less) able to jump from rock to rock, the developer had to continually adjust their strategy and retest their assumptions to make sure that the next person could cross safely. An API is like a bridge that is built across the stream. It doesn't matter if the water rises. It doesn't matter if the person crossing is an athlete or a child. They enter at one side of the bridge, and their path is clearly laid out to get them safely to the other side.

Where investment strategies involve new application software or new system integrations, specifically ask if your investments are taking advantage of the high leverage world of Cloud, SaaS and APIs.

Intelligent Data

Information – known these days as data – is at the core of why you invest in technology. A simple example shows how critical data can be:

> To estimate a person's income, we can start with the global average, or about $15,000 a year. If we know that the person is American, our estimate jumps to the average US per capita income, or $56,000. If we know that the individual is a 55-year-old male, the estimate jumps to $64,500. If that guy works in the IT industry, it jumps to $86,000. And if we know that the person is Bill Gates . . .[5]

Each additional piece of data can provide a more precise view of the situation.

Important Foundations

Your company has been gathering and storing information either since they started or since the start of business computing. A lot of the challenges with data come down to the fact that you have probably been collecting it for a long time. Old data and data stored in old systems can cause unique challenges. In the late 1990s and early 2000s, data started piling up at a tremendous rate in even the smallest of companies. It became a badge of honor to gather, augment and store large amounts of data. The investment value, however, became increasingly unclear. Business leaders thought they were spending money to improve their ability to use the data, but they were just investing to store more and more of it.

Before you approve any large investment decision, you should understand exactly what you are investing in. For reference and basic vocabulary, Figure 1.5 explains the actual parts of the computer system.

Data accuracy – A focus on data creates a new challenge—namely, making sure that the data is correct. It is not uncommon to have accuracy issues and gaps, but you should understand the reason why. Explanations include:

- *Where the data came from.* Until recently, systems were not integrated, so data came from disparate sources. How data is put together can cause a mismatch.
- *Timing.* Often data is updated at different intervals, so it is not always the most recent. In addition, adjustments are made at critical times like the end of a month or the end of a quarter, and different timing of updates can create gaps.

The thinking part, otherwise known as *capacity* or *CPU* (Central Processing Unit), is the computational speed with capability measured in GHz (gigahertz). The journey from Atari's pixelated stick figures to today's crisp, hyper realistic graphics demonstrates the growth in computing power. The risks to your strategy in the thinking part of the computer are:

- Speed – it cannot think fast enough.
- Smart – it isn't flexible enough.
- Age – older computers may simply be unable to do what newer technology demands.

The remembering part, otherwise known as *memory*. If you don't have enough memory, you cannot hold on to specific information or images. Growth in how much computers need to remember is exponential. The memory-driven risks to your strategy will be capacity and cost.

The algorithm part is the *programming*, which is how the computer is told what to do. A lot of time and money can be wasted chasing solutions that are not what was actually needed. The risk to your strategy will be making sure that the people building the algorithms understand the outcome you are after.

The data part is the *output* that makes the investment worthwhile. Whether it is tangible data that is being used, or data that generates productive outputs like manufacturing, there is always an output. The output-risk to your strategy is that what needs to be delivered is not well understood before money starts to be spent on the programming.

Figure 1.5 The Four Parts of a Computer

- *Definitions.* There are often multiple terms used to describe different items. Different assumptions of which data to use can cause gaps.
- *Gamesmanship.* Accounting and reporting regulations have reduced the likelihood of another Enron, but

operational decision-making can still impact the results being reported. Management of data to show a preferred operational view is a particularly troublesome gap.

Directors must be vigilant about whether decisions are being made on accurate data. Refer to Chapter 9, Oversight, for ways to address the challenge of legacy systems and historical data sources.

The Data Opportunity

Shazam *is a British software development company. They created an app that can "hear" a short sample of music or a script, and identify the music, movie, advertisement, or television shows that the clip comes from. The power of data for Shazam's core business is obvious – they store a tremendous amount of digital content, and the app matches the sample in just a few bars of music or lines of script.*

But that's not the most valuable part of the business model! Shazam can also predict which songs will be "a hit" as much as 33 days ahead of the song topping the charts (Knibbs, 2013). They use predictive analytics based on years' worth of record sales data. Shazam is effectively delivering entirely different products based on the data asset that they have developed.

There are many examples in which the data is the business. For example, think about consumer loyalty programs. Digital loyalty programs gather data about the member's behavior and analyze the data to offer relevant value to each individual member. They use the aggregated data to develop insight about the customer's preferences. They predict what campaigns will work with that customer in the future.

Data will not be a new line of business for everyone, but directors need to strive to make the best use of data for their business and invest in those opportunities.

There are two observations that should guide your data strategy:

1. **"It is not how much data you have, but what you do with it that counts."**[6] No matter how much data you have, if you don't use the data to see patterns, trends, and gaps, it isn't adding value. The right data does not magically happen; you must set out to build it.
2. **"The right data usually beats a better algorithm."**[7] Get in the habit of asking clear questions so simple algorithms can give you a high degree of confidence in the result. Complexity is counterproductive—the more complex the algorithm, the more assumptions are being made about both the data and the desired outcome. Focus on common sense and the ability to understand what the data is telling you.

Start by keeping it simple and making sure that you understand the questions:

- Treat data as a supply chain:
    - If the data you are getting seems too complicated, keep asking questions until you understand what it is telling you.

  - If data seems too compartmentalized, identify the integrated view you expect to see, and keep asking questions until you get it that way.
  - Expect to see data that supports operational leverage.
  - Do not give up; demand that your business understands the data so you can leverage it.
- Expect insight, not data in isolation or without context.
- Expect external data sources to increase leverage and add value.
- If you ask for analysis, communicate why you want it. Be clear on the questions you want answers to (rather than specifying what data you want).
- Recognize that the first time you see data, it may not be right—there will be timing and definition gaps.
- If you really need complex data analysis, you need to invest in a strategy, the skills, and the tools:
  - Recognize that giving an analyst a tool does not make them a data scientist.
  - Democratizing data analysis can be useful, but it can also simply add to the confusion and complexity.

The power of data starts with having the people, process, and technology in place to make productive use of it. What will drive value is keeping the focus on getting good answers to the right questions.

Other Transformative Technologies

Between the core dynamics, new technologies continue to emerge and can be a source of confusion or distraction. To help you assess if they can add value, and when you should be factoring them in, this section will discuss:

- Artificial intelligence (AI)
  - Autonomous vehicles
  - Computer vision and language processing
  - Machine learning
  - Robotics (RPA)
  - Virtual agents
- Block chain
- Brain–computer interfaces (BCI)
- Customer relationship management (CRM)
- Enterprise resource planning (ERP)
- Machine to machine (M2M)
- Intelligent software

Artificial Intelligence (AI) –Artificial intelligence is the ability of a machine to perform cognitive functions normally associated with humans. AI functions can include perceiving, reasoning, learning, problem solving, exercising creativity, and interacting with the environment.

Cognitive function (thinking) does no good unless you can act, so AI is never an investment focus on its own. It is always partnered with other technology, to deliver an action that will make it impactful.

Examples of AI in real-life applications include (but aren't limited to):

Autonomous vehicles – Application of AI plus sensing technology, to instruct the car to take action.

Computer vision and language processing – Application of AI plus assistive capabilities to understand sights or sounds and apply cognitive capabilities to respond.

Machine learning – Application of AI plus access to data to build and apply new algorithms for action (IBM's Watson is a working example of machine learning in action, bringing massive amounts of medical data together and formulating insights to assist doctors in diagnoses).

Robotic process automation (RPA) – Application of AI plus software and hardware to do manual, labor-intensive analysis and analytics. (Depositing a cheque from a cell phone is an example of RPA, where digital recognition of data like signatures combines with the ability to know where to look in the image and then "read" handwritten information such as a dollar amount. The deposit is accepted and moved on for processing without human intervention.)

Virtual agents (also known as "chat-bots") – Application of AI plus problem solving and learning, to identify the person on a call, interpret the nature of the inquiry, respond to the situation, and transfer the call to a live agent where appropriate. Sophisticated chat-bots are even able to sense a high degree of hostility or frustration and transfer a call to a real agent more quickly.

AI is complex and can be costly. Investment should have specific applications and measurable outcomes. AI is a good place to consider a pilot project or a prototype, or to partner with a provider with proven AI experience. AI investments should allow for validation of the potential before major investments are committed.

Block chain – Block chain is a record-keeping idea that maintains unique/secure access and keeps the data immutable. It is a concept more than a product, so we'll use an analogy to make it easier to understand.

Think of block chain as a system of lockable filing cabinets linked together with built in copiers and pneumatic tubes. The cabinets automatically copy the files as they are stored. Then they securely send multiple copies out to other cabinets through the pneumatic tubes. The system is designed to securely store many copies of the same file, spreading the copies over the many connected cabinets. You can get your file back from any of the cabinets, but you must have the key, and the file must be exactly the same in all the places before the system will let you remove it.

To translate, the filing cabinet is the "block." It lives in the digital world (rather than in the physical world) and is secured by encryption. As with a filing cabinet, the data being stored can be a document, a record, or even cryptocurrency.

The interconnectedness between the cabinets, the pneumatic tubes, represents the "chain." The chain sends and manages the multiple copies of the data between the cabinets.

As with unlocking a filing cabinet, data is placed in a block by a "transaction.' The person who puts the data in the block needs to have their own unique key to put the data in the block, and to take the data back out. That key is encryption, a random string of bits designed to scramble and unscramble data when the right key is presented. It provides the block chain security.

Once data is placed in a block, the block chain copies it out for secure storage in multiple other blocks. Then, when you want to take the data out of the block, the block chain platform goes and checks all the places it stored copies, to make sure that all the copies are still the same. If a copy in the chain is different, you cannot remove that data from anywhere in the chain. That is your immutable data.

When a block-chain platform is developed, the programming defines the blocks and chains. The block chain can also apply rules for how to adjudicate if any of the copies of the data do not match. The block-chain developer is building those adjudication rules, so skill and integrity are critical. If a difference is detected between stored copies, the rules can identify the need for some intervention, or they can define specific blocks to be more—or less—reliable and judge the discrepancy accordingly.

Let's look at a couple of real examples of block-chain platforms, to help make sense of it:

- Governments and document registries are using block chain to secure a registration record—for example, a land deed. In this example, a registry office has the encryption key to store a properly executed deed, and the legal owner of the property has the encryption key to get access later. When the property is sold, the owner's key combined with that of the land registry authority provides access to execute a property transfer. Then the new owner takes over the encryption key. The assurance that the deed is the proper record of ownership comes from the fact that the deed has been replicated to many locations, and that all the copies match.
- Fisheries are using block chain to track the movement of their product, so they can be sure of continuously safe shipping conditions. When the fish is packed, a temperature sensor is placed in the container, and tracked in a block-chain platform. The sensor securely records the temperature at defined intervals or checkpoints and maintains a block-chain record of the shipment's temperature status. The security of the block- chain platform ensures that the tracking cannot be broken and that the records cannot be modified along the way. The temperature data is then available at the receiving end of the

shipment, so the buyer has confidence in the freshness and safety of the product.

- Diamond and gold companies (including Berkshire Hathaway Inc.'s Richline Group) are working with IBM to develop a block-chain-based system—called TrustChain— which will track the origin of jewelery to ensure that it is ethically sourced. It is expected to be available to the public by the end of 2018.
- A private, nonprofit organization is working on building a global decentralized identity system based on block-chain technology. Partners include US-based IBM, as well as Deutsche Telecom AG's innovation group (Telekom Innovation Laboratories). The result will be immutable identity and citizenship records, which will benefit both security and immigration processes.
- Container shipping lines have teamed up with technology companies to upgrade the vast databases tracking cargo, moving away from reliance on millions of paper documents. The industry last undertook significant change in the mid-twentieth century, with the move to standardized containers. Success in cargo tracking will demand participation by manufacturers, banks, insurers, brokers, and port authorities around the world. If it works, documentation that currently takes days will be done in minutes, in most instances without the need for human intervention.

Block chain presents a powerful global opportunity that is industry-agnostic. Do not be distracted by the market focus on bitcoin and other crypto currency. The market excitement that was experienced in early 2018 had nothing specifically to do with block chain; block chain was just the tool used to create the product.

Block chain is not for everyone. If scale, flexibility of access, or security of access source is important, block chain might be a disruptor in your sector. On the other hand, it is a relatively slow processing method so not well suited to very large volumes where speed is important.

Block chain is also complex, which makes your system highly dependent on the integrity of the design. If you think that it might be relevant, consider configurable tools from reputable providers like IBM and Oracle, which would give you an auditable solution. Consider getting skilled help. Use a pilot project to test and decide if block chain should be a bigger investment focus.

Brain–computer interfaces (BCI) – BCI uses encoded information from a computer to send messages that can be understood as human neural activity. The most prominent example is cochlear implants, which convert sound into electrical signals that can be recognized by the brain. More dramatic examples use implanted electrodes, such as devices implanted in the arm of accident victims to generate hand and arm movement.

Thousands of Parkinson's patients are benefiting from BCI implants for deep-brain stimulation therapy. Advanced procedures also include stimulating the visual cortex to help the blind, re-forming neural connections to help stroke victims, and electronic monitoring to respond to signs of depression.

Broader applications are also starting to appear, ranging from thought-to-text typing to Elon Musk's vision of a full-on upgrade for the human brain. With enough time and investment, all those scenarios are highly probable. Cost and time to market will be the prohibitors.

The underlying barrier for BCIs is that the implants need to interact directly with neurons in the brain to be effective. Right now, it takes a drill to the skull to have a viable connection. Short of life-threatening or irreversible degenerative situations, it will take time to get past the scientific, technological, and commercial barriers:

- **Scientifically**, we know relatively little about the human brain, so experiments on humans still push the limits of our knowledge, and our willingness to accept them.
- **Technically**, it is not possible to send high-quality signals through layers of bone and membrane. Alternate channels, like reducing the size of implants, wireless technology, ultrasound, and magnetics are all being tested to improve the range of technical capability.
- **Commercially**, there are many practical barriers in getting medical devices approved for distribution. Presumably consumers won't be lining up for brain surgery. On the other hand, procedures like laser surgery for eyesight

correction were once considered an extreme step. Now laser surgery is ubiquitous. It seems to be human nature to come around to some dramatic procedures if we can expect dramatic results.

BCIs are market-making investments, rather than casually additive to something you do. If you are in a sector where there truly is an end game, test the logic with care to make sure that the outcomes can realistically make the market you are envisioning, in a timeframe that you can afford.

Customer Relationship Management (CRM) – CRM is an approach to manage a company's interaction with current and potential customers. CRM systems help identify unique customers, map relationships among them as appropriate, and manage interactions with each from a single source of the truth (database). CRM is real now and represents best practice for managing information about customers, partners, and suppliers, including history and relationships. The data collected in a CRM system can improve business relationships and enable growth by supporting analytics and behavior modeling.

Readers under 30 will find it hard to believe, but there was a time when the biggest risk in a sales organization was that a salesperson could leave their job and take their clients' business cards with them. Then the company was left to scramble to rebuild the customer list. A CRM replaces your sales team's Rolodex, giving you line of sight to and control over your customer list.

A CRM can contribute to strategic outcomes like segmentation and retention and, combined with data from social and mobile platforms, it can provide the foundations for transformative growth. CRM has also become the buzzword for the discipline of managing customer interactions and data throughout the customer lifecycle.

Enterprise Resource Planning (ERP) – An ERP is business-management software that lets you collect, store, manage, and interpret data from across interconnected business activities. The term is often used incorrectly to refer to a general ledger (G/L) system or more general accounting software.

Used correctly, the term refers to a system that integrates the business view of resource management including final tracking in financial-management systems. An ERP is a powerful strategic investment, because it supports and integrates core processes:

- Tracking business resources – cash, raw materials, production capacity.
- Tracking the status of business commitments – orders, purchase orders, and payroll.
- Managing workflow to integrate processes such as purchasing, inventory, sales, marketing, finance, and human resources.
- Automating back office administration functions, like accounts receivable (A/R), accounts payable (A/P), invoicing, and collections.

In addition to integrating processes, an ERP provides a single-source-of-the-truth view of data across multiple computerized functions. A truly integrated ERP uses common sources of data, with the same data being shared and used throughout the system.

When first developed, ERP systems were used in large manufacturing companies. They could efficiently integrate supply chain, warehouse management, and sales order processing with financial accounting and reporting. ERP moved into a broader business base as developers began to also integrate people resources through human-resource systems, and they began to have application in other industry sectors to manage a fulsome view of business processes. By the mid-1990s, ERP vendors addressed all core enterprise functions.

ERP solutions continue to grow in relevance because they deliver to the promise of an end-to-end process and a single view of data. End-to-end, known as E2E, is a philosophy that eliminates as many middle layers or steps as possible to optimize performance and efficiency in a process or system.

As an example of genuine business transformation-using systems, a CRM and an ERP can come together to provide an end-to-end process from "lead" to "cash":

- The first conversation with a customer is captured in the CRM – that is the lead.
- Discussions of price and terms are captured in the same system, tied to the lead.

- When an order is processed (in the same system and from the original lead), the contract is generated automatically by the system to align with the terms discussed.
- Raw materials are captured at receipt (or even at order), A/P is generated, and the resources are aligned with a cost-of-goods-sold accounting view of the product.
- Product or service manufacture is tracked in the business workflow.
- Delivery is confirmed in the system, and invoices are triggered.
- Funds received are accounted for against the relevant order in the same system. That is the cash.
- Customer inquiries, order follow-up, and delinquent accounts are all managed with the most current available view of the customer activity and order, in the same system.

Tracking all aspects of the revenue-creating transaction through an end-to-end process, using an ERP system, delivers financial integrity and operating efficiency.

An emerging trend in ERP systems is the ability to interact with other companies' ERP systems. For example, when a banking portal allows a customer to go online to directly order cheques, the bank is connecting the customer directly with their supplier by integrating their own enterprise system with that of the cheque provider. Passing the order all the way through to the cheque provider makes it convenient for the customer, reduces the risk of errors in handling the cheque order, and reduces the staff time required to support the account.

ERP solutions continue to extend functionality, including integrating new functions like compliance management. They also improve operating leverage and the quality of data, by streamlining process-based operations. An ERP can be a good strategic investment to address legacy system issues.

M2M (machine to machine) – Machine to machine is the term that describes direct communication between digital devices, without human intervention. Common applications often include industrial instrumentation, such as a sensor in an assembly line that recognizes multiple parts reaching the point where machine assembly can be completed. A more common example would be a car brake system that senses an obstacle in the road and automatically slows or stops the vehicle regardless of driver action.

Intelligent software – Intelligent software is software that uses Artificial Intelligence (AI) in the pursuit of defined processes or goals, delivering outcomes without human intervention. There are many examples of intelligent software:

- Software that can play chess or an online game would be considered intelligent software.

- IBM's Watson uses intelligent software to determine what medical examples relate to a specific case, and to decide what information to present to the doctor. For example, Watson analyzes more than 30 billion data elements to form genome sequences and is able to recommend customized cancer treatment for a single patient. One person's genome takes up about 100 gigabytes of memory, so this analysis would be an impossible task for a human.

- Recent advances of Watson go one step further – providing medical recommendations. For example, the Nutrino App Powered by Watson lets a pregnant woman register with the app, input her pregnancy status, dietary needs, health goals, food preferences, eating habits, and even data culled from wearable devices like Fitbit. She can then ask Watson a variety of questions about pregnancy, such as "What should I eat to help with heartburn?" Watson searches through Nutrino's database, which contains over 500,000 foods and 100,000 medical sources, and applies deep learning to tailor the answers to the individual.

- Netflix uses intelligent software to analyze your viewing habits and recommend other shows that you might enjoy; humans built the algorithm to match movie classifications and criteria, but that is the end of the human intervention - the software applies the business rules and makes thousands of recommendations a day, driving 75% of Netflix's viewer interaction.

- The utilities that monitor your email environment for spam and viruses are using intelligent software.
- Software agents, including robots and chat-bots, use intelligent software to deliver complex customer service functions. "Bots" engage with human-like qualities such as natural language understanding, speech and personality to reduce or eliminate staffing costs. The unique nature of software agents, as defined by the term "agent" in their name, is that they are software has the authority to decide which, if any, action is appropriate.
- Virtual assistants like Apple Siri, Google Assistant, Amazon Alexa, and Microsoft Cortana are also software agents. These markets are expanding rapidly, moving toward value-add partnerships – for example, Alexa is partnering with Toyota to provide an in-car virtual assistant experience.

Investment in intelligent software, as with AI, requires clarity of purpose and outcome.

* * *

According to Accenture, since 2000 some 52% of Fortune 500 companies have gone bankrupt, been acquired, or ceased to exist as a result of disruptions in their industry by digital business models.[8] Your investment levels need to align with the potential for digital technologies to impact your sector. Use the Smart Questions in Figure 1.6 to understand your technology foundations and to consider new opportunities.

Smart Questions to Understand Your Technology Foundations

- Do we have technology that is a differentiator or provides leverage?
- Who is looking at "what technology might be relevant" and reporting back to the board?
- What is our three-year technology investment plan? Are we investing in the pilot projects and foundational things to be ready for our next important investment?
- What decisions are we making now that will limit our options in three years?

Social Engagement
- How do we use social media, and what are the benefits and risks of that strategy?
- What are the metrics /results associated with our social media investment?
- Who is responsible for and what is our social media response policy?
- Do we create and curate sharable content?
- Do we share or sell our customer insight?

Pervasive Technology
- Do our mobile and pervasive technology strategies help or hinder our profile in the market?
- What mobile or pervasive capability might be unique or compelling for our business?

Global Capability
- Does our technology strategy position us for flexibility and scalability?
- What are the gaps between our systems strategy and our five-year targets? What are we doing now to bridge those gaps?

Intelligent Data
- Is our data giving us leverage or is it holding us back?
- How difficult is it for our operating entities to get- and trust- the data that they need?
- Do we have the foundations, tools and skills that we need to make data work for us?

- What are the three most important technologies that we see our competitors investing in?
- What are the three most important technologies that we see our suppliers investing in?
- What technology integration are suppliers or customers asking us for that we can't deliver on?
- What are our three next most important technology decisions?

Figure 1.6 Smart Questions to Understand Your Technology Foundations

Notes

1. *Complete Guide to Measuring Social Media ROI* (blog post), Statusbrew (December 13, 2017), https://blog.statusbrew.com/track-social-media-metrics-and-social-media-roi/.

2. https://www.marketingdive.com/news/how-urban-outfitters-leveraged-location-marketing-for-a-75-conversion-gain/436943/.

3. A. Betts, "The New Era of Personalization: The Hyper-connected Customer Experience," *MarTech Today* (January 23, 2018).

4. *Mobile Fact Sheet,* Pew Research Center (February 5, 2018), http://www.pewinternet.org/fact-sheet/mobile/.

5. T. H. Davenport, *Big Data atWork: Dispelling theMyths, Uncovering the Opportunities* (Boston: Harvard Business School Press, 2014).

6. "Digital Business Era."

7. E. Linask, "Social Media Is Responsible Business," *The Free Library* (January 1, 2012).

8. "Digital Business Era."

Chapter 2

Risk

In 2016, the Consumer Financial Protection Bureau (CFPB) levied a fine of $185 million, the largest in its history, against Wells Fargo in response to a evidence that millions of accounts were created without customer consent. Wells Fargo blamed the cross-selling scandal on a poor sales culture, identified remediations underway, paid the fine, and prepared to move on.

A year later, the bank accidentally leaked the personal information belonging to over 50,000 accounts.

At about the same time, it was revealed that the bank charged 800,000 customers for insurance that they did not need.

In the same year, the bank wrongly charged homeowners fees to lock in mortgage rates.

The Federal Reserve got involved and assessed the persistent issues to be the result of a fundamental failure of governance and oversight. They imposed unprecedented sanctions on Wells Fargo, preventing them from growing beyond their 2017 holdings.

Market Summary > Wells Fargo & Co
NYSE: WFC
56.00 USD +0.35 (0.62%)
Jun. 11, 10:28 a.m. EDT · Disclaimer
1 day
5 days
1 month
1 year
5 years
Max
70
60
50
40
44.28 USD Sep 30, 2016
2014
2015
2016
2017
2018
Open 55.79
High 56.04
Low 56.71
Mkt cap 272.91B
P/E ratio 15.67
Div yield 2.79%
Prev close 55.66
52-wk high 66.31
52-wk low 49.27

Source: New York Stock Exchange

Wells Fargo settled with regulators in April of 2018 for nearly $1 billion.

The multiple sources of scandal for Wells Fargo were known to the front lines and management at least 6–12 months prior to disclosure. The scandals were 100% preventable. The bank is now considered the poster child for failure of enterprise-level risk management, as a result of not being able to demonstrate any oversight or governance. Companies must now:

1. Disclose their approach to manage risk.
2. Demonstrate board-level knowledge of material risks down to the front line

In addition to the fine in 2016 and the settlement in 2018, Wells Fargo reimbursed harmed customers.

Although its share price recovered somewhat on an upside in earnings in Q4 2017 and Q1 2018, they continue to be challenged based on news of the industry-record settlement and continued systemic problems including a lawsuit by the USAA for patent violations.

The case of Wells Fargo takeaway ➔ Boards need to trust but verify that business risks are well understood, and that risk decisions and mitigation strategies align with the board's expectations.

Figure 2.1 The Case of Wells Fargo

The case of Wells Fargo, as discussed in Figure 2.1, makes it clear that boards have clear responsibility for gaps in risk management. Every regulated trading environment now operates under clear regulations for governance – in the United States, it is SEC rule 33-9089. Robust risk management programs are critical to avoid financial and reputational damage.

There are two clear trends:

1. **Regulations follow industry events**
   As shown in the timeline that follows, legislators try to get out ahead of the risks. Further, as new risks are identified we can expect that the more impactful an event, the more rigorous the legislative response will be.

   For example:

   - Stringent Payment Card Industry (PCI) standards followed reported incidents with Heartland in 2009 and Sony PlayStation in 2011.
   - In the wake of Facebook's mishandling of user information in 2018, US states are passing new regulations to address both privacy and consumer trust.
   - Bills before the US Congress in 2018 include the Cybersecurity Disclosure Act, which requires boards to either have the requisite skills or to identify their strategy for obtaining the advice and support that they need.

   The timeline shown in Figure 2.2 aligns events since 2002 with the regulatory developments.

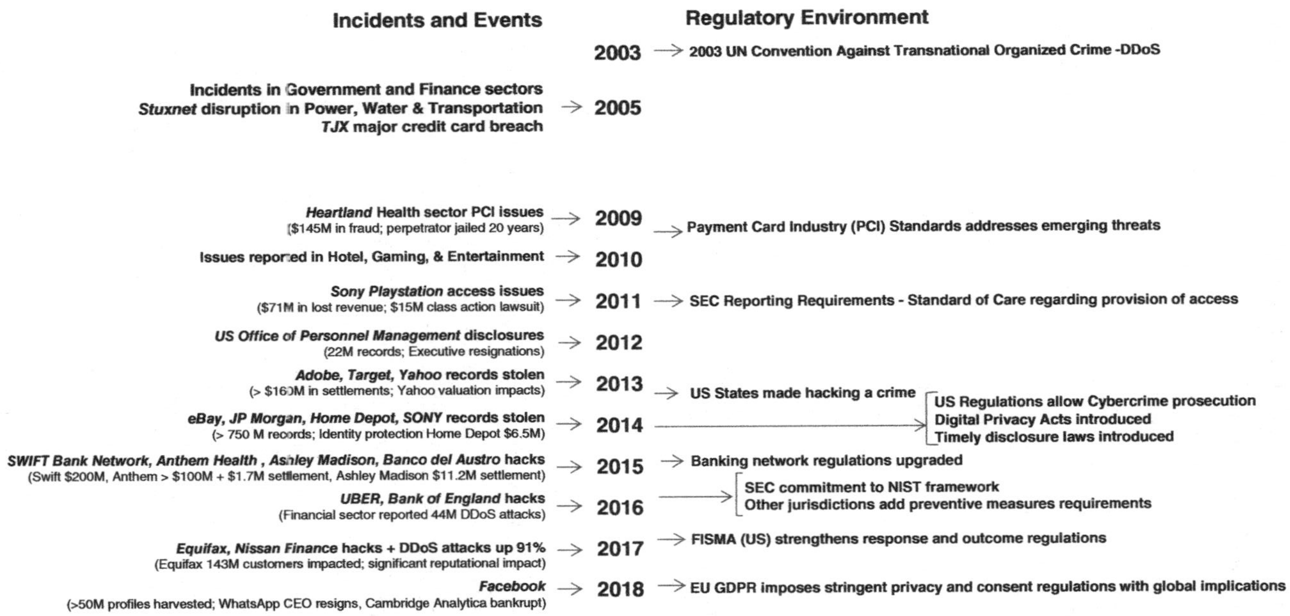
Incidents and Events
Regulatory Environment
2003
2003 UN Convention Against Transnational Organized Crime -DDoS
Incidents in Government and Finance sectors
Stuxnet disruption in Power, Water & Transportation
TJX major credit card breach
2005
Heartland Health sector PCI issues
($145M in fraud; perpetrator jailed 20 years)
2009
Payment Card Industry (PCI) Standards addresses emerging threats
Issues reported in Hotel, Gaming, & Entertainment
2010
Sony Playstation access issues
($71M in lost revenue; $15M class action lawsuit)
2011
SEC Reporting Requirements - Standard of Care regarding provision of access
US Office of Personnel Management disclosures
(22M records; Executive resignations)
2012
Adobe, Target, Yahoo records stolen
(> $160M in settlements; Yahoo valuation impacts)
2013
US States made hacking a crime
eBay, JP Morgan, Home Depot, SONY records stolen
(> 750 M records; Identity protection Home Depot $6.5M)
2014
US Regulations allow Cybercrime prosecution
Digital Privacy Acts introduced
Timely disclosure laws introduced
SWIFT Bank Network, Anthem Health , Ashley Madison, Banco del Austro hacks
(Swift $200M, Anthem > $100M + $1.7M settlement, Ashley Madison $11.2M settlement)
2015
Banking network regulations upgraded
UBER, Bank of England hacks
(Financial sector reported 44M DDoS attacks)
2016
SEC commitment to NIST framework
Other jurisdictions add preventive measures requirements
Equifax, Nissan Finance hacks + DDoS attacks up 91%
(Equifax 143M customers impacted; significant reputational impact)
2017
FISMA (US) strengthens response and outcome regulations
Facebook
(>50M profiles harvested; WhatsApp CEO resigns, Cambridge Analytica bankrupt)
2018
EU GDPR imposes stringent privacy and consent regulations with global implications

Figure 2.2 Alignment of Incidents and Regulations

2. **Regulations are getting broader and penalties more significant.**

The new EU General Data Protection Regulations (GDPR) took effect on May 25, 2018. The regulations define personal information as anything used to directly or indirectly identify a person. They require overt consent for sharing of data, including:

- Consent must be clear and distinguishable.
- Request for consent must be intelligible and easily accessible.
- The purpose for which the data will be used must be attached to the consent.
- It must be as easy to withdraw consent as it is to provide it.

The legislation affects companies in business transactions with the EU, including non-EU residents participating in EU governed boards. The impact is relevant globally. Fines are significant – the higher of either 4% of revenue or € 20M. The first few violations will be dealt with swiftly and to the full extent of the regulation. In the long term, global regulations are likely to align.

Indications are that an early GDPR target for fines will be Facebook, as a result of the data breach announced on September 28, 2018. The privacy regulator is looking at fines of as much as $1.63 billion if they are found to have violated the regulations.

There are three unique risks that have been exacerbated by technology and can impact a director's ability to meet their obligations to the corporation and its shareholders:

1. The risk of *specific liability* because of a data breach or operational failure. This risk category is known as ***cybersecurity***.
2. The risk of *general liability* because of gaps in risk oversight. These general business risks can be assessed and addressed by an ***enterprise risk management*** (ERM) program.
3. The risk of *litigation* because of what is deemed a material misrepresentation, otherwise known as ***securities fraud***. This is an emerging risk, but the financial and reputational exposure is significant, so directors need to understand the areas of exposure.

The three chapters that follow specifically address those three areas of risk. The Smart Questions in Figure 2.3 address your overall regulatory context.

- Who is responsible for monitoring regulations that are relevant for our business?
- How are new or changing regulations integrated with operational management?
- Are there any regulations where we are uniquely or knowingly exposed?

Figure 2.3 Smart Questions – Risk

Chapter 3

Cybersecurity

In September 2017, Equifax announced that a data breach affected 146 million US customer records. The breach allegedly occurred in May 2017 as a result of a security flaw that was known in March but not adequately fixed.

Equifax' share price has still not recovered, and shareholders have been rigorous in their litigation as a result. Claims include:

- Failure to protect the data system
- Failure to maintain adequate monitoring
- Failure to maintain adequate security
- Materially false and misleading reporting

In addition, Equifax executives sold about $2 million worth of shares before the breach was disclosed.

Market Summary > Equifax Inc.
NYSE: EFX
+ Follow
125.43 USD +0.36 (0.29%)
Jun. 14, 3:59 p.m. EDT · Disclaimer
1 day
5 days
1 month
1 year
5 years
Max
150
100
50
92.98 USD Sep 15, 2017
2014
2015
2016
2017

Source: New York Stock Exchange

Nearly half of all Americans were affected by the Equifax breach. It has become the poster child for the fundamentals of cybersecurity.

The case of Equifax takeaway ➔ As a matter of both policy and practice, invest in sustainable cyber security basics. Look for proof that best practices are applied to prevention, detection, and mitigation, so predictable problems are avoided and emerging issues are responded to quickly.

Figure 3.1 The Case of Equifax

As evidenced in Figure 3.1, cybersecurity is evolving. Consider developments over just the past two years:

- Based on 2016 estimates, large companies are worse off by an average of $200 million after a breach. As an example, when Yahoo sold its web services business to Verizon, it had to give a discount of $350 million due to the leak of data.[1]
- A 2017–2018 survey found that cyber-based ransom attacks have increased to match the value of cryptocurrencies. According to the report, the top driver of cyber attacks is now financial gain rather than nuisance, and attacks are becoming more targeted. Globally, 42% of companies experienced ransomware attacks, a 40% increase from a 2016 survey. Other key findings of the report include:
    - One in four businesses report experiencing cyber attacks.
    - Distributed denial-of-service (DDoS) attacks grew 10%, hitting nearly two in five businesses.[2]
- The average website connects to 25 other (potentially insecure) sites for content, such as video clips or advertisements.[3]

Whether you are on a public or private board, in a for-profit or not-for-profit sector, you need to spend time considering three key areas:

1. **Prevention and detection** – How do security mechanisms, automation, and education need to evolve to protect you?
2. **Planning** – Are you doing the right things?

3. **Mitigation** – What are you doing to avoid or offset impacts, and how would you respond to a breach?

Prevention and Detection

Cybersecurity best practice combines and balances security mechanisms, automation, and education. You need to ask questions that are specific enough to either confirm that controls are in place or to take a call to action for improvement. The right things to do fall into three categories: mechanisms, automation, and education.

Mechanisms – There is a well-defined set of things that you need to have in place, in use, and effectively monitored or enforced. Specific things to look for include:

Mechanism	What You Need to Know
Policies and procedures	Policies and procedures are clear standards for internal behaviour and the employee's role in protecting business assets from outside factors. Look for policies that are simple, clear, and straightforward, so they will be well understood. You should be able to read the policy and understand it.
User authentication and access control	User authentication and access control should be a routine part of how your systems are managed. That needs to include regular monitoring for any unusual activity and periodic audit to verify that the rules are being followed. Oversight needs to include: **1.** Both physical and logical access. **2.** Specific levels of control, so any sensitive data is explicitly restricted to the people who need it.

(*continued*)

Mechanism	What You Need to Know
	3. The recognition that some data, and some assets, warrant more security than others
Firewalls, anti-virus protection, and patch management	Firewalls, antivirus protection and patch management continue to be the essential foundations to protect your business. Your audit committee should expect certification that the environment has: • Firewalls, to ensure that bad things outside your environment cannot get in. • Virus protection, to ensure that if something evil gets into the environment it is contained and identified for action. • Patch management, to keep you up to date when major vendors and suppliers have identified new threats.
Monitoring	Monitoring lets you detect unusual activity in your environment and take action. One of the big gaps in the Equifax example in Figure 3.1 was the fact that they did not know they had been breached. Your team should be able to identify any unusual activity. Action should be taken, and issues should be reported as part of your risk oversight.
Data protection	Data protection demands that you: **1.** Know what data can be considered sensitive. **2.** Know exactly where that data resides. **3.** Know that it is secure.

Mechanism	What You Need to Know
	Tools like firewalls and encryption should be used to avoid instances in which sensitive data could be exposed.
General business security	General business security helps you to avoid known cybersecurity risks. Your program may include restrictions on: Access to potentially insecure external websites, which can be a source of viruses or other malicious capability. Access to potentially inappropriate external websites when there would be reputational risk if the access were revealed Access to potentially insecure utilities, like Dropbox, potentially opening an access channel or enabling smarter social engineering for phishing. The ability to send sensitive or proprietary information from inside the company to outside parties, circumventing internal controls and enabling employee-based exposures for theft or breach of privacy. These restrictions protect employees and the company from inadvertent cybersecurity risks.
White hat verification	White hat verification (otherwise known as penetration testing) is a critical sanity test for your overall controls program. It should be undertaken periodically regardless of the size or nature of your business, and results should be part of cybersecurity oversight.

(*continued*)

Mechanism	What You Need to Know
Automation	Automation speaks to the sheer speed and capacity of technology, which makes it critical to automate your security management. Your security team needs to proactively know where there is high-risk activity, so they can act before damage is done. For example, an unusually high volume of activity on your network could indicate a denial of service (DDoS), which could block your network and impact your entire business. Automation lets your security team know right away, so they can isolate that part of the network. A Network Operations Centre (NOC) provides real-time monitoring, so the team knows at a glance if anything needs attention. Look for evidence of proactive monitoring and plans to improve oversight over time.
Education	Your first line of defense is always going to be education. All employees need to take their security responsibilities seriously, and they should recognize their personal accountability. Challenge your CIO to make the program personal, impactful, and practical (not technical). Look for evidence of internal testing for appropriate employee knowledge. The board should be provided the security training given to each employee – you'll know right away if it resonates.

There are ways to prevent most cybersecurity exposures. The challenge for the board is to know that they are in use. The opportunity for the board is to acknowledge the activities and investments that are specifically required for an appropriate security posture, and to then demonstrate sound "nose in, fingers out" discipline to ensure that the right attention is being paid.

Planning

The most difficult cybersecurity decision you need to make is whether you want to just do what you need to do, or whether you want to proactively plan for the risk to your business. Global research shows that more than half of companies experienced a global data breach in the past five years, and half of those breached companies had more than one incident.[4]

The nature and breadth of exposures to plan for grows every year, as exemplified by the following notes. Not being proactive will put you at risk.

New levels of integration with suppliers and business partners create new risks. Supplier integration is becoming ubiquitous:

- Manufacturers integrated with suppliers
- Consumer products companies with integrated logistics
- Utilities and telecom providers with service providers

The new dependencies and contractual requirements need to align with your business practices.

The Internet of Things (IoT) is introducing a new type of exposure. Cars that can take instructions electronically rather than from the driver in control, stoplights and signal systems that are managed remotely, and computer-managed utilities, such as power grids and hydro dams, all present new opportunities for disruption. Planning is critical for those involved in a sector in which digitization is redefining operational controls.

The cost of a breach is significant. Costs include:

- Public relations demand of a crisis response
- Regulatory responses, including fines, legal fees, and litigation
- Forensic technical investigations
- Customer breach notifications
- Consumer protection programs as part of a strategy to re-gain customer trust

Given that you still must plan for and invest in cybersecurity after the fact, you might as well do it right in the first place. A proactive response will protect directors and officers from the litigious situations discussed earlier.

The hidden cost of a breach is estimated to be 90% of the total impact.[5] Companies that have experienced a breach report residual cost as much as two years later. Hidden costs include operational disruption, increased cost of capital, loss of customer and provider relationships, devaluation of trade name, and loss of IP.

Cybersecurity is getting more complex. Risks have moved beyond internal disruption and financial risk. Recent cases raise reputational risk as an equal if not greater concern, with examples including:

- Leaked internal communication (Sony)
- Internal (sometimes unrecoverable) data loss resulting from cyber events (SWIFT Banking Networks)
- External data loss including critical privacy breaches (Facebook)
- Intellectual property breaches (SONY PlayStation).
- Hijacking of information and assets for financial gain (City of Atlanta)

A cybersecurity plan is most effective if it is part of your overall technology strategy, rather than an add-on. It requires a continuous focus on base security measures as well as new exposures arising from the strategic changes. The bar goes up every year, so annual planning and budget cycles should include proactive cybersecurity improvements.

Response

Every year we see new security breaches. Notable examples include:

- 2013 – Adobe, Target, and Yahoo
- 2014 – JPMorgan Chase and Sony
- 2015 – Ashley Madison

- 2016 – Uber
- 2017 – Equifax
- 2018 – Facebook, Saks Fifth Avenue

These unfortunate examples keep coming. In each instance the quality and speed of the response made a difference in the customer response and regulatory decisions. Delays and obfuscations contribute directly to the reputational and financial impacts that a breach has.

In 2018, Facebook's multiday delay in responding to a major data breach undermined their customers' good will. To make it worse, Zuckerberg's misread of public sentiment meant that almost any response was going to be wrong. History leaves clues; given the nature of his business, he should have been better prepared.

There are ways that you can be prepared – and survive – a cybersecurity issue[6]:

1. **Get help.** Isolate the specific issues that you might face and frame your cybersecurity strategy so in the event of an issue you are able to respond as well as possible. Be prepared in advance.
2. **Engage expert counsel and pay attention to your insurance.** No single legislation or regulation will fully govern any issue, and the regulations change constantly. In the event of a breach, you need a response that is situationally appropriate and legally correct. Your insurers can identify a best practice place to start and can mitigate the highest risk scenarios.

3. **Designate a single point of contact for response and decision-making.** Your internal team will investigate and provide information, but in the event of a significant incident, the board should play a role. Simple decisions in advance, such as who has the authority to advise regulators or investors, set you up for success with a single decision-maker and a single communicator to manage you through an actual situation.
4. **Have a communication plan in place and have communications essentially prepared.** Delays in communication will undermine even the most effective response. Be prepared with both plan and content.
5. **Don't wait for perfect information before you respond.** Regulations are getting increasingly stringent about notification of privacy breaches. You will lose the patience of a cynical public and press if you delay. Pre-planned communications frame contextual items quickly, so you can be transparent by revealing what you know.
6. **Be fact-based**. Do not say something that you do not know to be true. Share the facts as you have them. Be genuine in disclosing the work you are doing to get more information. Include fact-checking in your pre-planned response structure to make sure that you do not have to correct information later; that only exacerbates skepticism. Do not make things up for the sake of something to say.
7. **Trust the team**. Plan a response structure and approach, and then trust the team. A blame-frenzy

will not solve anything and is certain to distract from your ability to respond. Only when the situation is fully resolved should you look for the team to provide a post-mortem review.

8. **Have remediation plans in place**. Your CIO should be able to provide foundational plans for people, process, and technology in the event of a breach. Look for evidence that the plans are defined and tested to support the overall response and communication plan at the board level. Plans should define who does what when, and (depending on the situation) how.

9. **Lead with remedies to customers**. Plans should include call center scripts and clear communications of responsibility and protection. As an example, recent cases have demonstrated that credit-monitoring services are a satisfying response in a privacy breach. If your business is actively managing highly sensitive customer data, you may want to have arrangements in place. Do not delay in offering customer-focused assurances.

10. **Practice**. Expect the team to do at least one walk through of the plan. Whoever is the accountable board participant should join the practice sessions, and they should report back to the full board on the plan and their observations.

We can only anticipate so much crazy. Most people have become accustomed to some level of risk in the digital world, but there is no tolerance for a lack of preparedness in a response. Speed to respond is the key for a board to survive a cybersecurity issue.

Cybersecurity presents a gamma risk for every company. If you experience an issue, it will not take long for impacts to magnify. Cybersecurity should be discussed at a full board level at least annually, and your CIO should be able to give you an update in a way that you can understand. In the event of a breach, duty of care demands that you did your best to understand. Use the Smart Questions provided in Figure 3.2 to provide the right level of oversight.

- Are we doing what we need in order to protect our data, systems, environment, and business? How do we know?
- Are there any gaps we know about that we have decided not to address?
- Are others in our industry investing in a level of control that we are not matching?
- How do we learn about new cyber risks that are identified? What do we do to stay on top of emerging issues?
- Do we have effective (tested) employee awareness?
- Do we have a cybersecurity plan, and what are we working to improve?
- What cybersecurity improvements or problems will come from our current technology plans?
- Do we have a cyber incident response plan, including communications?
- Have we defined an accountable team and who is in charge?
- What are our remediation plans? Do we practice?
- What is the board's role in the event of an incident?

Figure 3.2 Smart Questions – Cybersecurity

* * *

Notes

1. N. Goud, "Cyber Attacks on Businesses Cost Investors & 42 Billion Loss," Cybersecurity Insiders (2016).
2. H. Landi, "Survey: 42% of Companies Have Experienced Ransomware Attacks," Healthcare-informatics.com (January 22, 2018).
3. A. DeNisco Rayome, "42% of the Most Popular Websites Are Vulnerable to Cyberattacks," TechRepublic.com (February 6, 2018).
4. M. Bruemmer, "Survey – Most Companies Ill-prepared for a Global Data Breach," The Experian Data Breach Resolution Blog (June 27, 2017).
5. D. Weldon, "How Much Does A Data Breach Cost? Here's Where the Money Goes," CSO (August 24, 2016).
6. S. Ragan, "10 Mistakes Companies Make After a Data Breach," CSO (November 13, 2013).

Chapter 4

Enterprise Risk Management (ERM)

Requirements for Enterprise Risk Management (ERM) were put in place by the SEC in 2010.

In 2015, it was reported that Volkswagen was knowingly sidestepping environmental compliance standards by programming some of their diesel cars to turn on emissions controls only when they were being tested.

Within days, Volkswagen was hit with more than 30 federal lawsuits and their share price dropped more than 40%. It still has not fully recovered.

VOLKSWAGEN (VW) VZ.
162.15 EUR -2.28 (-1.39%)

Source: OTC MKTS NY

Volkswagen installed software to dupe emissions testing equipment on 11 million vehicles. Affected cars included diesel models of VW, Audi and Porsche sold between 2013 and 2016.

The CEO was removed for not knowing about the emissions risk, and being negligent exposed Volkswagen to the maximum legal penalties.

A Netflix documentary has intimated that Volkswagen tested the diesel fumes on monkeys, with parallels drawn to the events of the Holocaust.

A US class action suit, representing approximately 500,000 owners, settled for $25 billion in 2016. The Canadian action moved to closure in 2018, with a proposed settlement of $290.5 million for the approximately 20,000 owners.

Many of the 2,000 US complainants who chose to proceed individually are progressing with settlements as Volkswagen continues to manage their way through the situation.

The case of Volkswagen takeaway → Whether you are considering issues of financial or business processes and results, technology makes it easy and efficient to obfuscate bad business decisions. An enterprise-wide discussion of risk gives the right-minded people in your organization the opportunity to raise concerns about regulatory and reputational issues.

Figure 4.1 The Case of Volkswagen

The case of Volkswagen, discussed in Figure 4.1, demonstrates the importance of understanding the risk implications of technology decisions. Enterprise risk management (ERM) provides a foundation for examining an organization's full portfolio of risks. As a result of the stringent regulations that align with ERM as a practice, there are many tools and professional services to help directors meet their obligations.

At a high level, ERM methods are used to understand individual risks that are faced by the business. They consider how risks interrelate and support validation of appropriate mitigations. For ERM to be effective as part of an overall governance program, a board must have overt conversations about their risk-tolerance level. Every incremental level of risk prevention comes at a cost, and not every preventive measure is necessary or even prudent. Risk and security professionals often tend toward an absolute, so it is critical that the board balance the threat against both the probability of an incident and their tolerance of the event. Mitigations, including insurance, may be an effective alternative to investing in costly prevention measures – this chapter will help you make those trade-off decisions.

Risk is not an absolute thing, but a derived value, considering:

- Threat – potential events that could be impactful
- Value or liability – the value of the asset that would be lost or the cost of a resulting liability
- Mitigations – the measures in place to prevent or minimize impacts

- Probability and risk tolerance – the likelihood of the risk event, considered in the context of the business's willingness or ability to absorb the outcome

ERM is a disciplined approach to consider a range of threats. It is a critical method to specifically understand and consider both what may be probable and a worst-case scenario. ERM methodologies assess the countermeasures that are in place to avoid or mitigate a loss and identify whether the residual risk is acceptable for the business. If the risk is unacceptable, an ERM program would identify actions to bring the risk in line with your level of tolerance. Overall, an effective ERM program provides reasonable assurance that the company can achieve its' objectives given the risks or threats identified.

The fundamental concept to understand is that risk is not something that can be assessed based on an absolute observation. It is derived as a combination of the specific threat and what could actually go wrong.

As an example to make it easier to understand, consider the Bald Tire Scenario.[1]

If someone was holding a relatively bald tire, and asked you if there was an acceptable level of risk in using it, you would probably say no – without additional information you would probably consider the risk high. If they then clarified that the intended use was to be tied to a tree for a child's swing, you would change your assessment and say that the risk was low. Treads don't matter for a tire swing.

Knowing that the tire is for a tree swing, not to be used on a car, risk analysis would have you now consider the size of the tree branch and the strength of the rope to be used. They are now the risk factors.

ERM is a broadly based discipline aimed at addressing both complexity and interdependency. It is a best-practice method that provides the foundation for governance in the context of risk tolerance. Figure 4.2 simplifies how risk is evaluated.

The value of a structured risk program is that it looks at both what the risk is, the primary risk factor, and what contributes to the risk or the secondary risk factors. An enterprise program identifies and then quantifies risks, so mitigation strategies can be defined accordingly. For example, as shown in Figure 4.3, the best way to mitigate against reputational risk is to show diligence and have a well-planned and executed response.

It is in any investor's best interest to expect to see an ERM assessment at least annually. Boards need to invest in it, and private investors should expect to see it discussed in annual reports or business plans. See the Smart Questions shown in Figure 4.4.

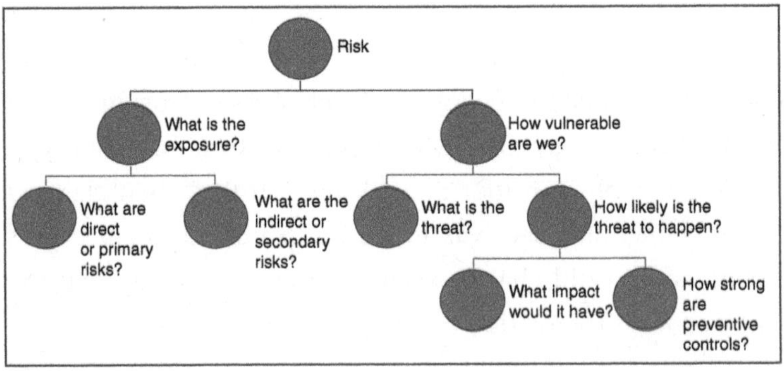
Risk
What is the exposure?
How vulnerable are we?
What are direct or primary risks?
What are the indirect or secondary risks?
What is the threat?
How likely is the threat to happen?
What impact would it have?
How strong are preventive controls?

Figure 4.2 How Risk Is Evaluated

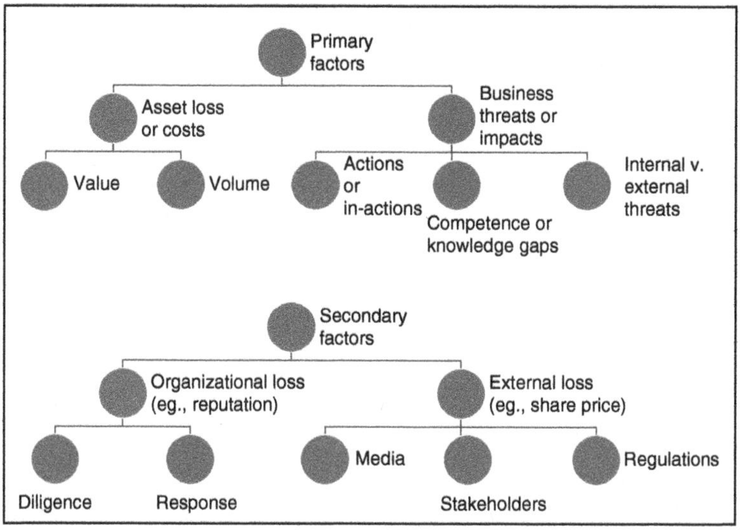
Primary factors
Asset loss or costs
Business threats or impacts
Value
Volume
Actions or in-actions
Competence or knowledge gaps
Internal v. external threats
Secondary factors
Organizational loss (eg., reputation)
External loss (eg., share price)
Diligence
Response
Media
Stakeholders
Regulations

Figure 4.3 Primary and Secondary Risk Factors

- Do we undertake an annual Enterprise Risk Assessment, and are the findings tested or validated?
- How is that assessment, and the resulting mitigation plan, presented to the board?
- Are there any currently known Enterprise Risks that have not been reviewed with the board?
- How do we facilitate right-minded people in the organization when they believe that they should raise a risk (what are our whistleblower policies)?

Figure 4.4 Smart Questions – Enterprise Risk

Note

1. J. Jones, "An Introduction to Factor Analysis of Information Risk (FAIR): A Framework for Understanding, Analyzing, and Measuring Information Risk," *Risk Management Insight* (2015).

Chapter 5

Litigation and Fraud Risk

In September, 2014, Home Depot announced that more than 56 million customer payment cards had been breached. There were three factors that made that announcement particularly alarming:

1. The exposure that allowed the breach was exactly the same as the one that exposed 40 million payment card records at Target in 2013, so the exposure was well understood and broadly communicated
2. In spite of the fact that there were relatively easy ways to significantly improve their security, Home Depot had not taken advantage of them to protect their customer card data
3. It was clear that the problem had existed, and not been detected, for about 5 months

By 2016, Home Depot announced that they were setting aside $161 million, not including insurance reparations, to cover the costs of the breach.

Disclosed payments in 2016 included $134 million to a consortium including Visa and Mastercard. There was also a consumer settlement of $19.5 million including a cash fund and credit monitoring.

An additional settlement in 2017 involved a payment of over $27 million to their bank partners. That settlement also included commitments to significant remediation to fix the known security issues.

Market Summary > Home Depot Inc
NYSE: HD
199.72 USD -0.58 (0.29%)
Jun. 14, 1:07 p.m. EDT · Disclaimer
Follow
1 day
5 days
1 month
1 year
5 years
Max
250
200
150
100
50
116.43 USD Feb 5, 2016
2014
2015
2016
2017
2018

Source: New York Stock Exchange

Home Depot directors and officers were named in derivative lawsuits. Although the suit was initially dismissed, it was recently settled to avoid an appeal.

The case of Home Depot takeaway → Duty of Care obligations now extend to cybersecurity oversight, and lack of understanding or knowledge is no longer a defense in the event of an issue.

Figure 5.1 The Case of Home Depot

Until the derivative lawsuits were filed, Home Depot's settlements were aligned with the traditional exposure of a data breach (see Figure 5.1). Suing directors on a cybersecurity issue is new. Arguments suggested that the directors and officers had not met their obligation for oversight and safeguarding. Not only had the company ignored a known industry threat, they did not have the most basic of controls in place to protect their payment card data. The situation was exacerbated by the time lag before they knew that they had an issue.

Cases like Home Depot have now taken the cyber exposure well into the realm of potential **securities fraud**. Until recently, a lack of Board level understanding or knowledge was a defense. Current cases show that can no longer be presumed. As with the Home Depot example above, directors and officers of ***Yahoo!*** and ***Wendy's*** have been named in derivative lawsuits for board failures ranging from failure to act to inadequate or misleading disclosures.

The case of ***Yahoo!*** is a recent example of litigation against the directors and officers of the company for the adequacy of the company's public disclosures. According to the plaintiff, the announcement of the breach jeopardized the pending merger with Verizon, resulting in Verizon paying $350 million less for the company; in January 2018, Yahoo settled its securities suit for $80 million.

The ***Wendy's*** litigation is more complicated, with shareholders naming specific directors and officers as well as the company. It alleged that the individual defendants *breached their duties of loyalty, care, and good faith* by *failing to* *implement and enforce a system of effective internal controls and procedures with respect to data security.* Among other charges, the suit suggested that Wendy's *failed to make full disclosure* of the effectiveness of the company's data security policies and procedures given the recognition that a security breach could adversely affect the company's business and operations.

Damages are not yet disclosed but known to include close to $1 million for the plaintiff's attorney alone.

Tested allegations of fraud to date fall into three categories:

1. **Companies that tout their data security.** Consider the case of ***Equifax***, who described their credit monitoring service as *delivering security*, and who over time emphasized *new security features*. Equifax's statements were considered *false and/or misleading* considering the undisclosed vulnerabilities. Complaints allege that the company failed to maintain adequate measures and failed to monitor for detection of breaches; as a result, their financial statements were materially false and misleading. The lawsuit against Equifax directors and officers specifically claims *breach of fiduciary duty*.
2. **Companies that (allegedly) said nothing about data security.** Silence has also proven not to be an option. Consider the case of ***Intel***, in which *the company knew their processor contained flaws that made them susceptible to breach, and failed to materially disclose*. At question is whether share prices were impacted by the lack of disclosure. This suit has not yet progressed enough to assess the implications.

3. **Companies that are not adequately specific in their disclosure.** Another recent case alleges that while ***Advanced Micro Devices (AMD)*** disclosed that data security was a known critical risk, *they did not disclose a specific flaw that (like Intel's) was a known exposure leaving them susceptible to breach.* As with the Intel case, at question is whether the board knowingly influenced share price by withholding information. The AMD suit is recent, but the suits are proceeding so appear to have merit. Whether disclosure specificity is a direct exposure is still in the process of being tested in the law.

Realistically, these examples are just the tip of the iceberg. Levels of disclosure, the nature of disclosure, and even the need for disclosure have become matters for potential litigation.

A fourth, untested area for allegations of fraud, may yet come out of the business of selling data and what comprises the necessary consent. The most notable example would be the recent events surrounding Facebook and Cambridge Analytica. Lawsuits have been filed, including filings against the board for breach of duty. Despite those pending legal actions, in early June 2018 it was disclosed that Facebook continued to strike custom data sharing deals with key clients, including Nissan Motor Co. and Royal Bank of Canada. Regulators are investigating, but boards need to think about:

1. Whether the data being purchased for use would pass a legal test of it being provided with consent.

2. Whether they, as the consumer of unlawfully acquired data, could be considered complicit with the data provider.

Incidents of data breach increased 164% between 2016 and 2017.[1] Data exposure is not just a big-company problem, and more than half of the reported incidents in 2016/2017 occurred in companies with less than 1,000 employees.

The average cost of a breach is US $225 per impacted record, without the added cost of litigation and legal settlements. Insurers in the EU are suggesting that the new and significant would not be covered in most policies, so attention to detail in both cyber insurance and directors and officers (D&O) policies is critical.

At the end of the day, a board's best defense is their ability to show diligence. Directors need to demonstrate *duty of care* in their oversight of cyber exposures and general business risks. See the Smart Questions in Figure 5.2.

- Do our data protection and cybersecurity procedures align with how we present ourselves to customers and partners?
- Do we have any known cybersecurity issues that we have not addressed? If yes, what are our plans to address the open issues?
- Have we overtly confirmed the requirements and coverage afforded by our relevant insurance coverage?
- Do we share, sell or consume any customer information without overt consent specific to the use?

Figure 5.2 Smart Questions – Litigation and Fraud

Note

1. *Internet Security Threat Report*, Volume 23, Symantec Corporation (April 2018).

Chapter 6

How Much to Invest – Digital Maturity

Compass Group PLC is a good example of knowing how much to invest.

Compass Group provides food services to a global market. Their focus on best-in-class execution is apparent in the fact that their revenue, profit, and earnings per share are all up over a four-year period, and their operating metrics including cost and safety incidents are down.

Business and Industry Accounts make up 39% of their revenue base. In the North American market, that division serves the large campuses of many major firms.

A recent guest experience survey at one of those campuses revealed that in spite of there being dozens of food venues and formats on the multibuilding campus, their guests universally felt that the options and variety were inadequate.

Market Summary > Compass Group plc
LON: CPG
1,622.00 GBX +19.00 (1.19%)
Jun. 22, 4:35 p.m. GMT+1 · Disclaimer
1 day
5 days
1 month
1 year
5 years
Max
1.800
1.600
1.400
1.200
1.000
800
2014
2015
2016
2017
2018

Source: London Stock Exchange

Deeper analytics revealed that their average guest would not go more than five minutes from their actual work location to pick up their lunch.

A traditional approach to the problem would have been to add more options at each venue. A more extreme response might have been to take on investment in more venues, replicating at closer intervals. Compass wanted to be more creative than that.

Instead, they looked to technology partners for ideas. They decided to offer a delivery program staffed with robots. They now offer any guest on the campus a robot-delivery option, providing frictionless access to all venues in a cost structure that made sense.

Compass did not start out looking for a cool place to use robots – they started with a customer problem and robots happened to be the right technology to solve it. Their mature use of technology investment shops in their share price.

The case of Compass Group PLC takeaway ➔Analytics allow you to be very specific about the problem that you are trying to solve. Then, you have the opportunity for technology to be part of the solution.

Figure 6.1 The Case of Compass Group PLC

Three things suggest that Compass Group (see Figure 6.1) is a digitally mature company:

1. They used the data they had to understand the real customer dis-satisfier.
2. Their assessment of alternatives included partner-based delivery models to manage the investment.
3. They solved the customer problem.

The fact that the solution was cool was a bonus.

Digitally mature organizations outperform their peers by 9% and are up to 26% more profitable. They deliver 12% greater market value.[1]

Your digital investment level is not just about how much money you think you are spending on technology, or how much your IT budget increases (or does not) on a year over year basis. It is about whether it makes sense to be a leader in your sector, or whether you can achieve the right results by letting others push the boundaries. There is no 'right' level of investment, but your investment level needs to be set by choice, not by default.

How much to invest, and your ability to transform when you need to, defines your digital maturity.

The Digital Maturity Model,[2] shown in Figure 6.2, is the general industry framework for understanding and validating your technology investment. Use this model to consider

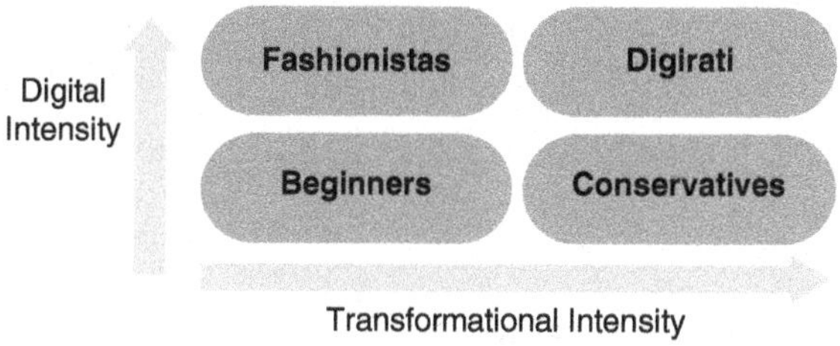
Digital Intensity
Fashionistas
Digirati
Beginners
Conservatives
Transformational Intensity

Figure 6.2 Digital Maturity Model
Source: MIT Sloan School of Management.

(a) what your current investment level means, and (b) if that is what you intend.

- *Digital intensity* (on the vertical) is the level to which you are investing in technology-enabled initiatives. Don't confuse digital intensity with being a digital or technology company – all industry sectors have leaders and followers in technology investment. Think of it as a measure of speed—how quickly is your investment letting you keep up with competitors or take the lead in your sector? What is your digital intensity, and what should it be?
- *Transformational intensity* is about your investment in the skills you need to deliver business transformation.

A Digital Beginner (the bottom left quadrant of the model) is a follower in both investment and transformation. It may be appropriate to be a digital beginner if you understand what it means, and that is where you want to be.

Being a digital beginner doesn't mean that you are not investing in technology. You may be very mature in the traditional sense of IT spending, in which case your systems are well managed and delivering to the needs of the business. You may even have some best-practice capabilities like a mature ERP. It simply means that you are investing based on the status quo.

You are a digital beginner if:

- Your investment (budget) is managed as a year-over-year run rate.
- Anything new in the budget needs to have a linear path to a defined business case.
- You are satisfied with starting small or lagging in your sector.

Being a beginner should be an intended investment strategy. Don't find yourself in this quadrant by accident.

Moving to the right in the model, we find the Digital Conservative quadrant. A Digital Conservative favors prudence over innovation[3]:

- You recognize the need to have a clear vision.
- Your investment level is aligned with your culture and governance.
- Your investments are well managed.
- You have transformational leadership in the business, but technology is more the enabler than the driver.
- You are probably either skeptical about new trends, or you have not seen the clear need to do something different.

The most significant risk for a digital conservative would be the long-term consequence of missing opportunities or not trying new things. You are probably placing a lot of reliance on your IT team to know what is good for you and to gradually incorporate the right things at the right times. If your investment level is in this quadrant, the onus is on you to make sure that you listen to your IT leaders – you have made them your conscience.

A Digital Fashionista, up at the top left, is willing to invest in technology but the focus is on what is new in the moment more than following an enterprise investment strategy:

- You recognize the need to test the boundaries.
- You are probably avoiding the pitfalls of spreading your investments too thin to have an impact.
- You may have initiatives that are outside the appropriate governance process and are causing distraction.
- You may not be leveraging what your CIO knows and can contribute.
- You may or may not be realizing value for your investments.
- Initiatives are probably pet projects of leaders in the organization rather than aligned with a defined strategy.

If you are a digital fashionista, you probably have maturity in some areas, but your technology function may be lacking in genuine enterprise governance or enterprise architecture.[4] It's okay to be a fashionista, as long as there is governance over what gets funded, and why.

Digirati are in the final (top right) quadrant because they have a demonstrated understanding of how to drive value. Think of Digirati as companies that apply an investment formula, as represented below, to their technology investments:

$$\text{Value-based investment} = \frac{\text{Vision} + \text{Governance} + \text{Engagement}}{\text{Investment}}$$

Aligning Your Investment Level with Where You Want to Be

There isn't a right or a wrong digital maturity; there is only alignment between where you want to be, and your investment level. Alignment lets you avoid gaps between intention and reality. If your intentions are clear and aligned with how you are investing, you can reduce the risk that you will be surprised by an industry disruption or that your shareholders' expectations will not be met.

Based on a 2017 survey, there is a measurable gap between board level concerns about digital disruption and their actual willingness to invest for transformation. Based on that survey, 82% of directors see technology innovation as an important challenge, yet 44% believe that they can still grow over the next 5 years without specific investments.[5] Close to 40% of those directors think their CEO and IT leaders have the right investment strategy in place at an operating level and they do not expect to increase their CAPEX commitments for technology.[6] If those directors are expecting anything to be new or different, they will be disappointed.

Studies also suggest that there is a gap between the CEO's view of reality, and that of their IT leadership. For example, 51% of IT leaders say they are unable to respond to the digital demands they face, yet 55% of these same IT organizations are working with the same or less money on an annual budget basis. Only 7% of CEOs say that their digital savvy is strong.[7]

It is important to ask critical questions, and to be assured that someone is thinking about your technology investment level, and your digital future. Directors, CEOs, and investors need to have an aligned view of what kind of digital investment they want to participate in. There are three steps you can take to make that decision:

1. Arm yourself with data so you have an opinion.
2. Talk to the CIO directly.
3. Benchmark your investment against competitors and the sector.

Use the Smart Questions shown in Figure 6.3 to calibrate your position in the digital maturity model. Go into your next strategy discussion with an opinion about where you are and where you think you should be.

Another way to keep the board discussions more engaged with investment value is to have a nontechnical board

- Do we consider technology a strategy, an enabler, an operating function, or a product?
- Do we have a digital advantage? If yes, exactly what is it?
- How much of our budget (OPEX and CAPEX) is spent on maintaining the current systems?
- How much of our budget (OPEX and CAPEX) is spent on growth or strategic initiatives?
- Who is responsible for understanding industry trends and reviewing them with us? Are those individuals proactive and intellectually curious?
- Are we lagging behind, keeping up, or ahead of our competitors?
- If we are lagging behind, what will be the consequence? Do we have plans to catch up with the sector?
- How do we prioritize technology resource use?
- How does management decide what investment discussions to bring to the board?
- How is our investment aligned with the board's view of strategy?
- Are projects evaluated on both $ and nonmonetary benefits?
- Are outcomes measured against our intentions?
- What are our current projects? How do they support our strategy?
- Does the board have enough direct contact with the people looking at our technology investment opportunities?

Figure 6.3 Smart Questions – How Much to Invest

member meet regularly with the CIO to talk about the issues of the day and report back on what resonates[8]. No offense to the technology person on your board, if you have one, but it is easy to fall into camaraderie where the technical director speaks for the others rather than genuinely pushing the envelope on the full board's need to trust but verify.

Finally, look for your staff to benchmark your investment against a couple of key competitors and your overall sector. Quarterly and annual reports are good sources of strategic insight. Supplier events and industry associations are a great source of insight. Your CIO should be responsible for monitoring and reporting on your competitor and sector investment profiles as an input to your strategic planning cadence.

In *Thinking, Fast and Slow*, Daniel Kahneman talks about the inside view,[9] in which "the realities of the outside world are sometimes replaced by people's extrapolation from their own experiences and data." Kahneman says this dynamic would hold true even when the people involved are attempting something they have never done before. The potential for poor decision-making cannot be underestimated.

In terms of technology investment, the implications are terrifying. You need to have opinions that are fact-based. Then you can be deliberate about your investment level.

> Directors are there to provide a perspective on the future that helps management identify those opportunities that are the most worth pursuing.
>
> **C. Bart, "20 Questions Directors Should Ask About Strategy," CICA**

Understanding your digital maturity lets you be more specific—not specific about what technology you need, but specific about what you aspire to be—so you can build the vision part of the value equation.

Notes

1. G. Westerman, D. Bonnet, and A. McAfee, "The Advantages of Digital Maturity," *MIT Sloan Management Review* (November 20, 2012), https://sloanreview.mit.edu/article/the-advantages-of-digital-maturity/.

2. Ibid.

3. Ibid.

4. *Enterprise architecture* is the strategic and integrative alignment of technology investment plans with a complete expression of the enterprise; Provides a master plan or collaborative force to align goals, vision, strategy, and governance in an executable framework that is agile enough to take advantage of new opportunities and stable enough to support operations, continuity and recovery.

5. *Director Lens, Survey Fall 2017*, Institute of Corporate Directors & Environics Research Group (2017).

6. Ibid.

7. D. Aron and G. Waller, "Taming the Digital Dragon: The 2014 CIO Agenda," Gartner Executive Summary (2014, no. 1).

8. C. Bradley, M. Hirt, and S. Smit, *Strategy Beyond the Hockey Stick* (Hoboken NJ: John Wiley & Sons, 2017), p. 71. Five ways to raise your game:
   1. Improve the quality of proposals.
   2. Engage in more collaborative, learning-oriented dialogue.

3. Experience more authenticity and rigor – challenge better.
4. Make less biased, better decisions calibrated against an outside view.
5. Lead your team with more courage, take calculated risks, and more vigorously commit.

9. D. Kahneman, *Thinking, Fast and Slow* (New York: Farrar, Straus and Giroux, 2011).

Chapter 7

How to Prioritize

From an all-time low in late 2013, BlackBerry shares are on a bullish run of late. There is speculation that share price could go over $40 by 2020, largely due to the prioritization of investments in their automotive division.

BlackBerry is leveraging its digital legacy in security, by applying it to the Internet of Things – including cars, trailers, and planes.

BlackBerry has commanded a significant market share in a very short time by launching two auto sector products:

Radar, which enables asset tracking for fleet assets like trailers and vans.

QNX, which is software that provides safety and security for electronic systems in cars, including autonomous vehicle systems.

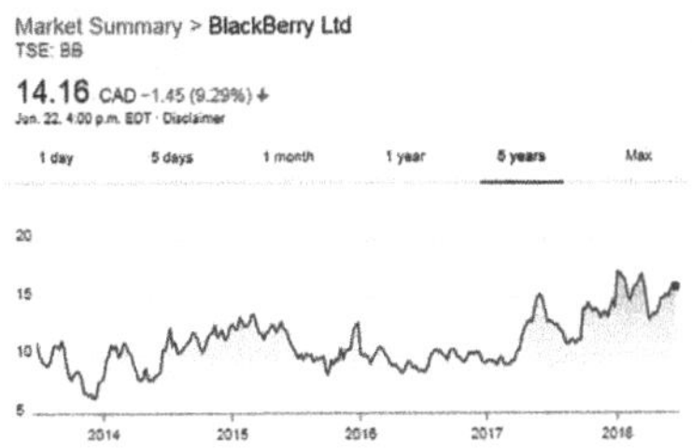
Market Summary > BlackBerry Ltd
TSE: BB
14.16 CAD -1.45 (9.29%)
Jan. 22, 4:00 p.m. EDT · Disclaimer
1 day
5 days
1 month
1 year
5 years
Max
20
15
10
5
2014
2015
2016
2017
2018

Source: Toronto Stock Exchange

Recent reports suggest that BlackBerry is also developing a security service that would remotely scan vehicles for exposures like viruses, and tell vehicles to pull over if they are in critical danger. Reports are that the service would be able to install security patches to an idling car, addressing the increasing auto sector vulnerability to hacks and takeovers. In 2015, two hackers exposed a vulnerability in Fiat Chrysler that led to the recall of 1.4 million automobiles in the United States.

After a devastating industry loss in 2013/2014, BlackBerry has taken the time to prioritize in alignment with its unique strengths. It is recovering. Instead of fighting to regain share in the mobile device market, they it looked at its strengths in the context of emerging technology trends. It now has identified a digital priority that will let shareholders.

The case of BlackBerry takeaway ➔ By staying focused on what your differentiators really are, you can leverage technology to push further into the opportunity to both save and create market opportunities.

Figure 7.1 The Case of BlackBerry

As shown in the case of BlackBerry (see Figure 7.1), a focus on your unique, differetiated market positioning is a critical part of your strategic planning. Prioritizing your technology investments is a simple extension of the strategic planning work you already do. It should not be a separate, disjointed process. The investments that you need to make should be an integral part of your deliberations on core business strategies.

It is not uncommon for strategy presentations to the board to be developed by the teams responsible for sales, with technology strategies tacked on to support the story. Look for overt alignment of technology investments and specific outcomes that with make a direct contribution to the business plan.

Ideally, board engagement in the conversation will enable clear and genuine technology strategies that build on your business priorities. Board-level technology strategy conversations can become an integral part of your current approach to planning. While you are thinking about market positioning, driving growth, or improving operating leverage, take a few extra minutes to talk about the technology investments that can contribute and gaps that might be impactful.

Start with Your Current Business Strategy

You are not investing in technology for the sake of technology. Your existing strategy is the critical point of reference, so incorporate the investments you need to make in your current framework. Consider what is out there that could surprise you, and talk about technology trends so you know that you are putting the right dollars in the right places at the right times.

As an example of how to identify transformational strategies, this chapter uses Porter's Five Forces[1] (Figure 7.2), which considers:

- Buyers or customers
- Competitors
- Potential new entrants to your market
- Substitute products
- Suppliers

Any proven planning model can work. The key is to overtly add technology drivers into your conversation.

Buyers/Customers

Almost every sector is experiencing disruption around customer engagement and expectations. By looking at the buyer/customer side of the model, you can move from whether (and why) they will buy more to talking about what your customer is trying to achieve with your product or service. Focus on outcome. Are you (or could you be) making a difference for their lifestyle? Will they engage with you because they know people who do? Are there things that would make it easier for your customer to use more of your service or product? If your customers are other businesses, can you save them time or money?

Consider Porter's Five Forces to Identify Digital Investments That Can Change Your Competitive Landscape

- What is the competition doing that could change the game?
- What's going on at the boundaries of your business model that could let the competition change the balance of power?
- Are there black swan events that you are uniquely positioned to be ahead of?

New Entrants Are a Genuine Risk

- Do new capabilities like Cloud make it easier for a new entrant to match your offerings? What is the biggest risk?
- How modern do your clients expect your offerings to be?
- How are you leveraging SaaS, API integration to deliver capabilities better, faster, cheaper?

Customers and Buyers Have Power

- What new leverage does your customer have?
- Think outcomes – What are buyers trying to achieve and what experience can you deliver?
- Does it improve your bargaining power if you make it easier to engage with you?

New Entrants
Suppliers
Competition
Buyers
Substitutes

Suppliers Become Partners

- Are there gaps or bottlenecks in your delivery model, where a partner could improve operating leverage through analytics or new channels?
- Where could a more partner-focused approach improve your offerings?
- Where could your channels, analytics, or operating processes benefit from quick access to best practices?

Delivering Experience Makes You Less Vulnerable to Substitutes

- How can you build a more holistic experience for your customer?
- Can sensors, wearables, pervasive devices, robotics, intelligent systems… have a positive impact on experience?
- How can you create stickiness with your client base?

Figure 7.2 How to Identify Transformational Strategies

Source: Adapted from Porter's Five Forces Model, Harvard Business School.

Think of the Burberry case (Chapter 1). Burberry's aspirational investment was to provide an immersive social shopping experience, because they knew from their analytics that would increase sales. They started with the customer side of the discussion and envisioned an entirely new kind of experience. In the Compass Group example (Chapter 6), by understanding the specific customer dis-satisfier, the company was able to invest in a specific program to improve its customer engagement.

It is important to think specifically about what your customer will value. Staying with a retail example, retailer Uniqlo invested in smart mirrors so the customer can put on a garment and have the mirror show them different colors. It seems that in-store customers value not having to take the garment on and off to make a color selection. If you don't offer the next 'best' experience, you may be uncompetitive.

Old school as it may seem in a digital strategy context, you may need to revert to mystery shoppers and mapping out your competitors' experience. On the buyer side of the five forces model, you need to be focused on the real change that consumers and business customers expect you to deliver. Then build an investment plan that drives that change.

The economy is moving toward buying experiences and outcomes rather than products or services. Your customer strategy must include developing the data acuity to measure and manage outcomes and commitments.

Competitors, Potential Entrants, and Substitute Products

The technology drivers for competition, potential entrants, and product substitutions are similar. They share the same three risks, so we will consider competitors, new entrants and substitute products together. There are four key factors to consider:

1. ***Barriers to entry*** – Technology is getting easier to access, and technology costs are moving to a pay-as-you-go model. The start-up cost of technology is no longer a significant barrier to entry. Digital service offerings, like Microsoft's cloud offering Azure, make it possible for a competitor or new entrant to engage highly secure, world-class capability with almost no lead time.
2. ***Ease of integration and extension*** – Cloud-based services can handle almost every operational function without any investment in building systems. Application program interfaces (APIs) reduce the time, cost, and risk of integration, to deliver a high functionality, robust business model. In the early digital world, it might have taken a new competitor time measured in months (even years) to be up and running, and even longer to be a threat. The new world beckons for smaller entrants or substitute products to quickly gain a foothold in your market.
3. ***Higher bar on standard processes*** – As with the earlier integration notes, the emergence of more standardized industry solutions means that your competitors and new entrants have access to a more streamlined and compartmentalized business model

without having to plan it out or build it into a system. The actual processing of data is no longer the endgame. Instead, the strategic opportunities are the data, the integration with other processes, and the extension of the tools for access and function.

4. ***The role of customized systems*** –Your executives may push for custom systems. Unless there are differentiators that your customers care about, you may be better off using standard tools and building uniqueness into the way you use them. It is almost always cost prohibitive to offer the kind of best-in-class capabilities (including social, mobile, and analytics) that a specialized industry solution would have offered.

The best way to specifically defend yourself against competitors and new entrants is to really listen to what your customers are saying. Focus on the experiences and outcomes that they will value, so you stay relevant and are ready to take on competitors, new entrants, and substitute products. Then share that insight with your CIO so they can identify the investments that will get you there.

Suppliers

One of the biggest opportunities for digital impact is with suppliers. An early industry example of supplier leverage would be in just-in-time (JIT), where heavy manufacturing was able to offset the cost of carrying parts inventory. A more recent example would be book publishing, where many books do not physically exist until you place the order on Amazon. Then they are printed on-demand at a facility adjacent to the Amazon shipping center.

The high leverage opportunity with suppliers is integration. By automating processes that are labor intensive, cost savings and operating leverage can be found in machine-to-machine (M2M) handling.

Examples of M2M include:

- **Direct supplier integrations** – Many bank portals now link customers directly to the providers of cheques and credit cards. The bank keeps the customer relationship and line of sight to the customer's activity, but they do not have to be in the middle of activity that can be automated directly with a third party.
- **Business process outsourcing** – Some mortgage providers can link directly with third-party providers for appraisals, land registry inquiries, and management of legal instructions. The companies that provide these adjacent services are disrupting their own industries, and they often provide direct M2M links to save valuable time and cost in processing.
- **Aggregation of suppliers to deliver a differentiated product** – Amazon aggregates thousands of third-party global suppliers who ship directly to customers, and they curate those suppliers by managing products, prices, and supplier ratings to gain significant cost advantages. In addition to offering thousands of unusual products without warehousing them directly, they enable a familiar customer experience for almost anything a customer could want.

Integration and aggregation with suppliers are real. The best way to assess this opportunity is to look at adjacent business models—such as new channels—to really understand what the opportunities are. The *Profit from the Core*[2] model can be used to extrapolate digital opportunities, as shown in Figure 7.3. Ask your management team to map out the adjacent-technology strategies and bring insight to help the board's oversight pertaining to the boundaries of your strategic framework.

Factor for Speed

Your computers manage large volumes of data and transactions at very high speed. Technology and speed are often presented to boards as risks, but according to Gartner, 56% of CEOs who are investing in digital transformation are seeing measured profit gains.[3] It is imperative that boards be aware of the risks, but they also need to look for the opportunities.

As evidence of the impact of speed, technology is frequently the driver in what are termed black swan events – that is, random events or occurrences that deviate from what is normally expected. A black swan event is unanticipated, but often, a little discussion and forethought would have made the situation significantly less random.

The rise of the personal computer is often cited as a black swan event. But was it really? Working in the computer industry in the 1980s, I knew people who were building their own personal computers. Paper-based memo processes

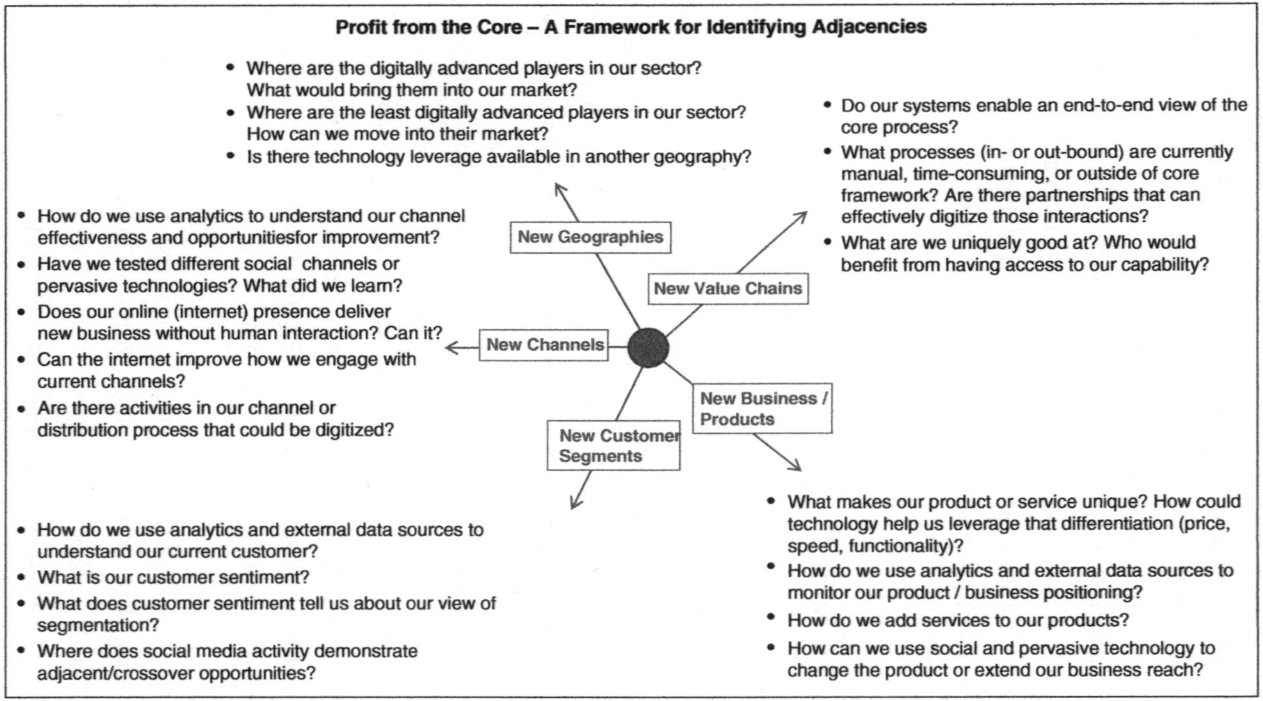
Profit from the Core – A Framework for Identifying Adjacencies
New Geographies
• Where are the digitally advanced players in our sector? What would bring them into our market?
• Where are the least digitally advanced players in our sector? How can we move into their market?
• Is there technology leverage available in another geography?
New Value Chains
• Do our systems enable an end-to-end view of the core process?
• What processes (in- or out-bound) are currently manual, time-consuming, or outside of core framework? Are there partnerships that can effectively digitize those interactions?
• What are we uniquely good at? Who would benefit from having access to our capability?
New Channels
• How do we use analytics to understand our channel effectiveness and opportunitiesfor improvement?
• Have we tested different social channels or pervasive technologies? What did we learn?
• Does our online (internet) presence deliver new business without human interaction? Can it?
• Can the internet improve how we engage with current channels?
• Are there activities in our channel or distribution process that could be digitized?
New Business / Products
• What makes our product or service unique? How could technology help us leverage that differentiation (price, speed, functionality)?
• How do we use analytics and external data sources to monitor our product / business positioning?
• How do we add services to our products?
• How can we use social and pervasive technology to change the product or extend our business reach?
New Customer Segments
• How do we use analytics and external data sources to understand our current customer?
• What is our customer sentiment?
• What does customer sentiment tell us about our view of segmentation?
• Where does social media activity demonstrate adjacent/crossover opportunities?

Figure 7.3 A Framework for Identifying Adjacencies

Source: Model adapted from Chris Zook with James Allen, *Profit from the Core: A Return to Growth in Turbulent Times* (Bain & Company, 2010).

were being replaced by early electronic mail systems. The pervasiveness that we see now may have been difficult to see then, but it is disingenuous to call the outcome random.

The book *Fooled by Randomness* states that a black swan event depends on the observer. For example, at Thanksgiving what may be a surprise for a turkey is not a surprise to the butcher; the objective should be to identify areas of vulnerability in order to "turn the Black Swans white."[4] By thinking through the adjacencies in your sector, and factoring in the effect of speed, you may be able to see the swans and make sure that they are white.

Four things can help you avoid technology-driven black swan events:

1. Know your own digital maturity, and continually revisit whether you are where you need to be.
2. Specifically consider the boundaries of your competitive landscape, including what is happening at the adjacencies. If your competition is actively hiring data scientists, for example, you may need to pay attention to how analytics and behavioral modeling could change the industry.
3. Pay attention to the influences at play with your buyers, suppliers, entrants, and substitutes.
4. Write down what scares you most. Be specific. Use ink, not pencil. Then share those fears with your board associates and your CEO.

Ask questions, have opinions, and talk about outcomes. None of us has a crystal ball but using a model for your

- What technology strategies are being recommended by senior management?
- Have we asked our CIO what they believe to be our biggest strategic risk or opportunity?

Customer

- What outcomes are our customers after when they consider our product or service?
- What would make it easier for our customers to use our product or service, or to use more?
- Can technology offer new ways for us to differentiate?
- Do our customers care about what other people or companies think of us?
- Can we acquire to improve our digital reputation or loyalty?

Sector

- What technology investments are being by our competitors?
- What are the emerging trends for our sector? Where are we at risk of being left behind?
- Have we benchmarked our product or service experience against our customers?
- What is being said about us, and our competition?
- Can we acquire to gain technological advantage?

Supplier

- Have we assessed our end to end process to know where processes could be improved with technology?
- Do suppliers use their technology to help us differentiate? Can they?
- How could technology improve the strategic value of our supply chain?
- Can we partner for greatness?

- What have been the most surprising recent trends or events in our sector?
- Who is advising us on potential technology-driven inflection points in the sector?
- What scares us most?

Figure 7.4 Smart Questions – How to Prioritize

strategic-planning work does help you think through what can be impactful.

The Smart Questions shown in Figure 7.4 will help you form opinions, both about whether your current priorities are right and about what your priorities should be.

Don't get caught up in the specific technology; think directionally. You are a director or CEO because you can filter through a lot of information and make decisions. Let your intuition and common sense guide you.

Notes

1. M. Porter, "Five Competitive Forces That Shape Strategy," *Harvard Business Review* (January 1, 2008).

2. C. Zook and J. Allen, *Profit from the Core: A Return to Growth in Turbulent Times* (Hoboken, NJ: John Wiley & Sons, 2010).

3. "Gartner Survey Shows 42% of CEOs Have Begun Digital Business Transformation," Gartner Newsroom (April 24, 2017).

4. N. Taleb, *Fooled by Randomness* (New York: Random House, 2010).

Chapter 8

Clarity

Visa Inc. is a good example of the value a company can deliver to shareholders by having clarity.

Visa started with a strong brand that is known for providing consumers with secure and reliable face-to-face payment processing. In the last five years, Visa has taken advantage of an infection point between the payment industry and technology, and it has strategically invested in both the ways to pay and the ways to be paid.

By recognizing the strategic value of its network, Visa moved from being the preferred provider for face to face transactions to being the preferred provider for e-commerce, government to consumer and business to business processing. It also bridged its capability over to the mobile space, by providing a secure backbone for the port-to-port transactions required for tap and other mobile payments.

Market Summary > Visa Inc
NYSE: V
135.33 USD +0.67 (0.50%)
Closed: Jun 22, 6:03 p.m. EDT · Disclaimer
After hours 135.33 0.00 (0.00%)
1 day
5 days
1 month
1 year
5 years
Max
51.25 USD Oct 10, 2014
140
120
100
80
60
40
2014
2015
2016
2017
2018

Source: New York Stock Exchange

With a strategic focus on taking the friction out of the payment experience, Visa had the clarity to invest in flexible capabilities that were of value for both the consumer and the provider. It avoided chasing one-off strategies for specific tactical markets, and instead demonstrated the maturity to focus on enabling a single set of standards that would deliver value across its platform and offerings.

The clarity of Visa's technology strategy shows in their share price.

The case of Visa takeaway ➔Taking a leadership position in an industry or supply chain creates new opportunities to transform the sector and to shape the company's position. Technology creates new opportunities for market changing competition.

Figure 8.1 The Case of Visa

As shown in Figure 8.1, the case of Visa, companies that find the confluence of investment level, focus, and priority are better able to develop clear digital plans. This chapter will guide you through turning your strategy into an executable plan. Figure 8.2 frames the challenge and the opportunity – how to find clarity in the eye of the storm.

Parts of this chapter may go deeper than you would like, but the devil is in the details. Successful digital directors recognize that clarity requires specificity, and that clarity will make their investments more successful.

There are four ways to improve clarity in your investment plan:

Vision – Make sure that everyone understands what you are investing in, and why.

Direction – Set boundaries for how you expect the investment to take shape.

INVESTMENT LEVEL
INVESTMENT FOCUS
CLARITY
INVESTMENT PRIORITY

Figure 8.2 The Perfect Storm Model

Time and scope – Balance your expectations so you get what you need when you need it.

Risk – Allow for what can go wrong

In the book *Strategy Beyond the Hockey Stick*, McKinsey talks about the importance of being bold.[1] In this chapter, we will focus on clarity as leverage for bold technology investments.

Vision

Think of vision as the "what" and "why" of your investment. It is the point on the horizon that you are steering toward. Bold strategies reinforce the need for clarity. You need to "get specific about where the opportunities are, so you can translate high level trends into investable pockets."[2]

> Vision without execution is a daydream.
>
> **Japanese proverb**

Digital investments will only be a differentiator if you are specific about the outcome you are after, and you can measure for success against those outcomes.

Years ago, I was helping a large transaction-oriented business plan for automation of ordering and fulfillment. The board believed that they were clear about the focus – improve processing time and compliance and deliver operational leverage through cost savings. Unfortunately, the board and CEO were reticent to declare the objectives for cost savings. The business units were focused on processing time and compliance as department-level activities. In the absence of clarity, they missed the operating leverage in integrating across their departmental boundaries. They established metrics around processing time, but they did not plan or measure for actual cost savings. The investment was suboptimized because the board was not clear about the outcomes they were after.

The best way to make sure that your vision is understood – and realized – is to align spending with outcomes. You will probably need to shift money away from some current spending plan to fund your digital investments; be clear about what you expect to be different.

Start by looking into how operational planning decisions are made with respect to technology investments. Figure 8.3 provides a transformation model that will help you address the unique requirements of technology investment planning.

If capital investment is a growth amplifier, there will be no better reinforcement of the vision than the redirection of scarce capital resources. Research shows that realigning more than 50% of your capital investment drives 50% more value over a 10-year period than if you do not.[3] Proactive directors need to ask questions about the strategy and outcomes behind capital investment plans.

Direction

If vision is the what and why of your investment, direction is the "how." Direction aligns your investment with the vision

Mechanisms	Enrich Your Technology Investment Planning
Planning Cycles	→ Include technology in your planning → Treat it as a journey, not an event → Support ongoing board / CEO dialogue with regular CIO briefings
Decision Making	→ Expect to be given meaningful options in major investments → Have a view of the Digital Ecosystem, and a Digital Strategy, to provide context for discussion
Strategic Focus	→ Chose investments where you can define outcomes–what will be different, how, and by when → Choose a small number of important initiatives
Budget Alignment	→ Focus on what moves will differentiate your business → Talk about the moves first, the budget second → Benchmark to measure outcomes
Best Practice Budgets	→ Move to spending 25% of your investment on transformation
Business Alignment	→ Incentivize the business for delivering to outcomes
Delivering Leverage	→ Incentivize business engagement in digital investments
Tactical Roadmap	→ Have a bias for action → Use pilots and partnerships to deliver specific outcomes

Figure 8.3 Enrich Your Technology Investment Planning

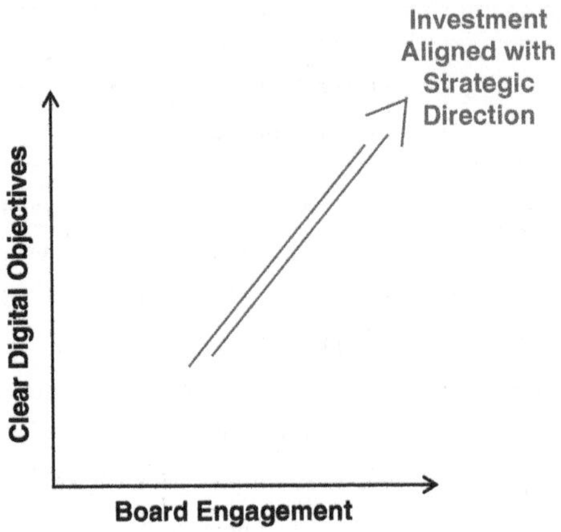
Investment
Aligned with
Strategic
Direction
Clear Digital Objectives
Board Engagement

Figure 8.4 Investment Alignment

by framing the steps to take or the path to follow. Directors need to be engaged in setting that direction to ensure that technology investments stay aligned (see Figure 8.4).

Your technology investment plan should drive from the overall business strategy, rather than being communicated as an afterthought. Ideally, the board would talk about technology early in their strategic planning work. Alternatively, the CEO can champion the development of a digital strategy, working iteratively with the board for strategic direction.

The board should look for the digital strategy and technology investment plans to be written down, presented as part of the board process, and overtly approved and governed.

Time and Scope

It does not help to be clear on what you expect to happen, and how that should be accomplished, without some context on when you expect results. Directors and CEOs often see time as a discrete element discussed in isolation from other factors. Then they are disappointed when expectations are not met. Time needs to be considered in the context of scope.

Your CIO lives every day with a framework that balances scope, time, and budget (see Figure 8.5). If any one of the three changes, the other two must adjust to keep the balance. Success demands that what is being delivered (scope) is tightly managed, so that the work can get done in the time expected. Successful boards and senior leaders overtly enable the trade-offs.

Boards and CEOs seldom say, "We tried to get too much done." Instead, the perception is generally, "They did not get it done by the committed date." Successful technology investment considers all three factors together, and an effective board expects schedule commitments to be met. This is an important area to practice a "nose-in-fingers-out" approach to oversight.

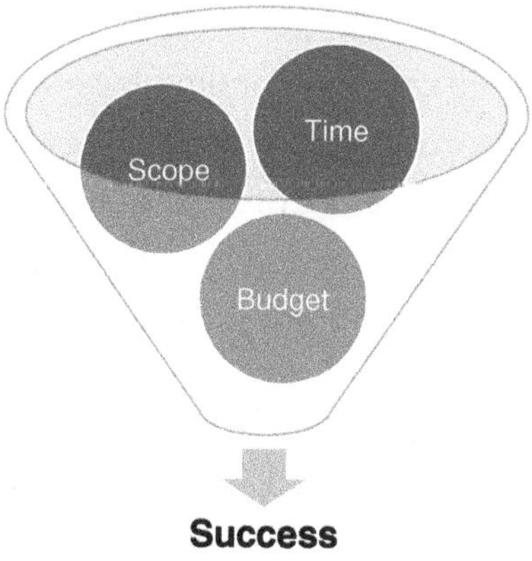
Time
Scope
Budget
Success

Figure 8.5 The Success Funnel

You may be dependent on the CIO to tell you how long the company needs to deliver on your strategic requirements. You are also entitled to have a sense of urgency and a notion of when you would like to see results. The guiding principle is to be reasoned and balanced.

Genuinely give your CIO the opportunity to speak to the challenges and opportunities, including:

- What resources need to be assigned to the work, and when they will become available based on current priorities.
- What would need to be forfeited to meet the required timeframe (is that a trade-off you want to make?)
- Other considerations around the timing of work – for example, changing your financial reporting process in the middle of a quarter or midstream in the fiscal year may create a data accuracy issue.
- Consider where the outcomes you are after are aligned with other operational considerations, and make timing decisions accordingly.

  The most common cause of time-based disappointments is the "time-boxing" of the delivery team to an outcome without considering scope. On average, your business staff will take a dictated schedule and do their best to meet it, but if they do not have the opportunity to genuinely align their work with your expectations they are unlikely to be successful. Instead of a strategic project being an exciting opportunity, it will become a stress-filled dis-satisfier.

Progressive improvement beats delayed perfection.

Mark Twain

Being clear on schedule considerations helps the business understand your vision. For example, if staff members know you want to have something to talk to shareholders about at the post-AGM reception, they can think in terms of what progress they can deliver, on that timeline that will resonate for the shareholders. If you are committed to delivering cost savings as part of your next fiscal budget approvals, they can focus on the specific and measurable parts of the strategy that can be extended into budget commitments.

If schedule discussions identify the audience and the impact you are focused on, you give the CIO and the staff members the opportunity to propose options that can align with your sense of urgency. Alignment on sense of urgency translates to alignment on both time and scope. It is a critical part of investment clarity.

Investment Risk

The final point of clarity for your digital investment is risk—not enterprise risk as we discussed earlier, but the risks surrounding investment uncertainty and the probability that things will go wrong.

> Risk is the clue that our dreams are both real and great.
>
> **Craig D. Lounsbrough**

Few digital strategies carry no risk, but with forethought either you can either address the risks and make them go away or you can make decisions that will mitigate the risks. Your CIO and project teams will know how to address or mitigate most risks, but they can only be effective if you foster a practical approach to risk management:

1. **Fail early** – Do not let the team treat risk as an afterthought. They should be able to articulate the investment risks, so they can understand, qualify, and mitigate the risk early in the work plan. Late-breaking risks are hard to recover from. Specifically:
   - If they need to confirm the technical viability of an idea, fund a proof-of- concept or pilot project to get answers. Do not expect your team to know if a technical project will work based on vendor demos and written specifications.
   - If they need to confirm the technical viability of an idea, invest "seed funding." Give your team the resources that they need to get the details right.
   - Do not confuse a pilot project (a test) with a gradual rollout. The difference is important. A pilot or test means that things will potentially be learned and that plans can be adjusted. A scaled-down launch or gradual rollout means that the deliverables are known to be right, but the deployment will be done over time. Executives often interpret a pilot to be a first step in a rollout, but it is not. Clarity on which approach is being taken is critical.
   - If your CIO identifies a potential risk for the project, ask them to be specific, and then give him or her the time and resources to get fact-based.
2. **Encourage honesty** – Oversight of transformational projects often involves charts that show a green, yellow, or red status as an indicator of the health of the project.

In theory, a yellow or red status should indicate that the project has an issue to be addressed, but most teams avoid showing governing bodies anything but green for fear of causing alarm. By the time an issue is flagged as red, the governing body has little ability to influence outcomes or address the risk.

Rules of thumb:

- Green means that everything is on track in terms of budget, schedule, and scope.
- Yellow means that there an issue, but it is understood and being addressed; it is flagged as yellow for transparency and awareness.
- Red means that there is an issue, but it is not fully understood and/or the actions to address the issue are not yet known or committed. If status is red, the governing body should be participating in a decision-making process that will enable movement back to yellow.
- An initiative should never go straight from green to red, or red back to green; if it does, the person running the initiative is withholding information from the oversight process.
- Test your understanding by discussing scenarios using "what happens if . . ." questions
- Risks should always be identified with mitigation options. Think in terms of a range of outcomes, rather than an absolute, to improve your understanding of what the risk really is and how to offset or self-insure.

Groupthink* occurs when the members of a highly cohesive group lose their willingness to evaluate each other's inputs critically.

Symptoms of Groupthink

- Illusions of vulnerability – Members overemphasize the strength of the group and feel that they are above criticism: This leads the group to approve risky decisions without addressing where individual members may have serious concerns.
- Illusions of unanimity – Members accept consensus prematurely, without testing whether all members really agree. Silence is often taken for agreement.
- Illusions of group morality – Members of the group feel that something is "right" and above reproach: Members feel no need to debate ethical issues.
- Stereotyping of the "enemy" as weak, evil, or stupid–Members do not realistically examine their competitors and they oversimplify competitor motives: The stated aims of outsiders, or their reactions, are not considered.
- Self-censorship by members – Members refuse to communicate concerns for fear of disturbing the consensus.
- Mind-guarding– Members take responsibility for ensuring that negative feedback does not reach influential members of the group.
- Direct pressure – In the unlikely event that a note of concern is interjected, the group responds with pressure to bring the deviance back into line.

Guidelines for Avoiding Groupthink

- Challenge every member of the group to be critical as an evaluator; overtly share objections.

Figure 8.6 How to Avoid Groupthink

- Make it clear that the leader or discussion chairperson is independent, and should avoid articulating a preference.
- Create subgroups to all consider the same problem; then compare the results.
- Facilitate additional information from the subordinates, peers and networks of group members; encourage briefing documents and direct presentations to the group.
- Invite outside experts to participate in discussions, including observing group processes.
- Assign a member to play devil's advocate at each meeting.
- Overtly focus on alternative scenarios.
- Once consensus is reached, reexamine the next (but unchosen) alternative, comparing it to the chosen course of action.

*Irving, L. Janis, Groupthink, 2nd ed. (Boston: Houghton-Mifflin, 1982).

Figure 8.6 *(Continued)*

3. **Avoid groupthink** – Many companies use some form of "new initiative" risk assessment, but these are only as good as the discussion that takes place to do the assessment. See Figure 8.6 for strategies to improve your risk evaluation effectiveness.

Your digital strategy and investment decisions need to provide the clarity that your business needs to deliver the outcomes you expect. The Smart Questions in Figure 8.7 will help.

- What is the point on the horizon that we are steering toward?
- What do we think our industry will look like in three to five years?
- What are our three most important technology initiatives? What will be different when each is successful?
- Which director is tasked with regularly meeting with the CIO?
- What timing trade-offs are being made that the board be aware of?
- What technology assumptions could impact our annual plans or budget?
- What technology-based strategic outcome would be bold?

Figure 8.7 Smart Questions – Clarity

Notes

1. C. Bradley, M. Hirt, and S. Smit, *Strategy Beyond the Hockey Stick* (Hoboken, NJ: John Wiley & Sons, 2017), p. 127.
2. Ibid.
3. C. Bradley, M. Hirt, and S. Smit, "Strategy to Beat the Odds," McKinsey Quarterly (February 2018).

Chapter 9

Oversight

In 2007, Loblaw undertook a major technology investment aimed at bringing together disparate processes by replacing legacy systems with an end-to-end SAP ERP platform. The initially three- to five-year plan took more than seven years to deliver. The final phase alone is estimated to have cost over $100 million in IT and customer service work.

Investor patience was challenged and share prices fell as skepticism grew.

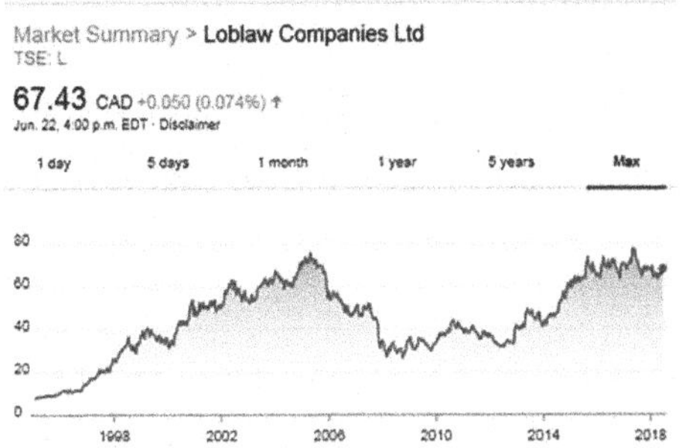

Market Summary > Loblaw Companies Ltd
TSE: L
67.43 CAD +0.050 (0.074%) ↑
Jun. 22, 4:00 p.m. EDT · Disclaimer
1 day
5 days
1 month
1 year
5 years
Max
80
60
40
20
0
1998
2002
2006
2010
2014
2018

Source: Toronto Stock Exchange

Sobeys undertook a similar transformation program, also experiencing significant delays, budget overruns, and schedule misses. The impact was also felt in the Sobey's share price.

Government projects are most notable for cynical news coverage of large-scale debacles, not necessarily because the government fails more than industry but because it is less able to cover it up and public funds are exposed.

The Canadian Federal Government and the Queensland government both had payroll systems that garnered global attention for their schedule and budget challenges. Both systems promised large savings that were not delivered. In both instances, experts were consulted and project risks were identified along with mitigation strategies that could have helped to salvage the situation. Incompetence, culture, and politics prevented those recommendations from being implemented.

The issues at Loblaw went on for too long and were too big to hide. Their failure to understand the issues facing the project was a failure of oversight. The impact on the share price was significant and endured until the project was completed.

Key takeaway ➔ Governance of large technology investments takes as much attention and oversight as investments in M&A or corporate expansion programs. Investors expect their Board to be paying attention, and they hold the company accountable for success.

Figure 9.1 The Case of Loblaw

So far, this book has focused on the investment choices you have – what to invest in, and how to make those investment trade-off decisions. You have prioritized to find the cash you need. You have identified the technology that you think could provide leverage or growth. You can focus your investments in the places that you will deliver value. You have a bold plan and have enabled your CEO and CIO to develop a clear and actionable digital strategy.

What can possibly go wrong? As shown in Figure 9.1, the case of Loblaw, many things can detract from even the best of digital investments.

Digital investment is one of the few places where a board and CEO are able to directly influence the outcome of your investment. It is as if you can buy a stock, and then be in the boardroom to make the decisions that will affect share price. Yet most boards do not realize their own ability to impact their success. Instead, they approve technology investments and then just hope it all works out. The phrase "eyes glazed over" comes up a lot when I speak to directors.

A hurricane does not just have winds that are spinning in circles. Remembering the Hurricane Irma example, there are also winds around the outside that can shift where the storm goes. Those winds can have a positive or a negative effect depending on your perspective.

There are similar influencers in technology and transformation investments. Those influencers can either be multipliers,

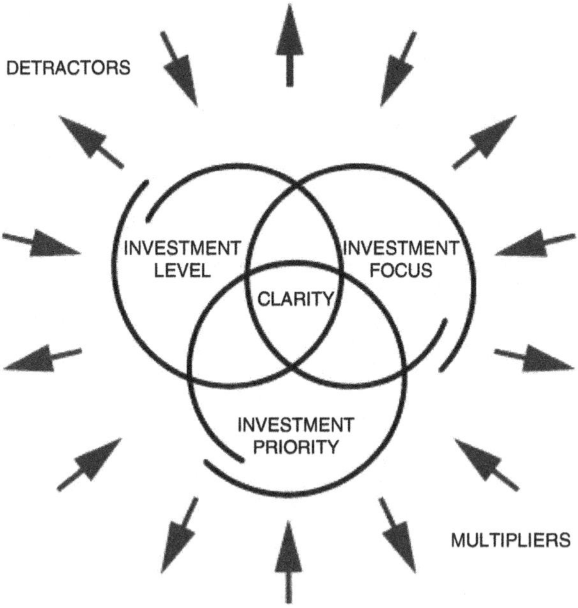
DETRACTORS
INVESTMENT LEVEL
INVESTMENT FOCUS
CLARITY
INVESTMENT PRIORITY
MULTIPLIERS

Figure 9.2 Detractors and Multipliers

helping to drive the initiatives and improve outcomes, or they can be detractors causing delays and overruns. As with the winds in the storm, Figure 9.2 shows how these key influencers can cause a project to fail.

A 2013 study by MIT Sloan[1] considered the factors that detract from the success of transformational investments, and found that absence of urgency, funding, accountability, and vision were the most frequent contributors to failure. In most instances, with positive focus and attention, those detractors can also be multipliers.

Recognizing the need for a board to be "nose in, fingers out," it is critical for directors to understand what the

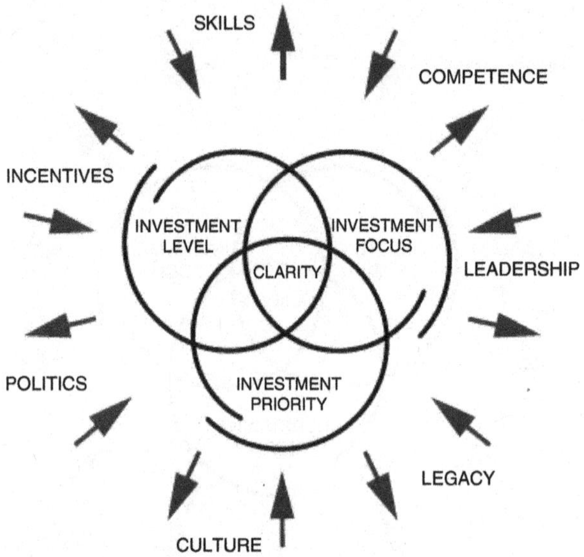
SKILLS
COMPETENCE
INCENTIVES
INVESTMENT LEVEL
INVESTMENT FOCUS
CLARITY
LEADERSHIP
POLITICS
INVESTMENT PRIORITY
LEGACY
CULTURE

Figure 9.3 Factors for Oversight

key detractors and multipliers are and how to engage in appropriate diligence. There are seven distinct factors (see Figure 9.3) where a director can appropriately ask questions as part of their oversight responsibilities:

1. Board and CEO competence
2. Organizational leadership and attitudes
3. Legacy technology
4. Culture of innovation
5. Organizational (political) challenges
6. Measurements and incentives
7. Skills

Board and CEO Competence

According to Korn Ferry, "Boards need to gain an appreciation for what the possibilities are, including how technology can help establish successful companies with needed transformation."[2] They go on to observe, "boards would never delegate financial responsibility to the CFO and then ignore it – why would they delegate their digital investment strategy and then not invest in having sufficient and relevant skills and understanding for proper oversight?"

Boards need to be competent to oversee digital change. Digital strategy and technology investment are good opportunities for boards to exercise a "*nose in, fingers out*" (NIFO) approach. Many boards establish a technology committee or add technology risk to the scope of a risk-oversight committee. Then, an outsider with the relevant skills augments the relevant committee. A technology expert on a committee can bring the board closer to the technology investment and establish expertise on a task-assigned basis.

Adding a technology committee or technology focus on the risk committee, rather than having genuine technology skill as part of the board, may be better than doing nothing, but there are three risks:

1. By adding digital competence as an external input, the board is still delegating the need for competence. If the board needs to address a crisis situation, the crisis can be fully materialized by the time that third-party expert can be consulted.

2. By adding digital competence as a committee-level role, the board misses having a digital perspective as an integral part of strategic decisions. Technology has value to add in almost every aspect of growth and profitability. If the board members believe that they have addressed their duty of care by establishing a committee, the risk is that they will never take the important step of having genuine digital competence in the boardroom.

3. If the external expertise is an augmentation of the risk committee, they will only enable more profound conversations once an item has been raised as a risk. This reduces the opportunity for technology discussions to be proactive in either investment or issue management.

If you believe the 2017 World Economic Forum assertion that "you either disrupt or are disrupted,"[3] delegation of digital strategy decisions is not adequate oversight. To be competent, directors need to assume responsibility for championing the digital culture, so the expertise needs to be present in the boardroom. Experts in *Leading in a Digital World*[4] suggest that does not have to mean recruiting a technologist as a board member. Strategies for an individual director can include:

- **Becoming a student of all things digital.** Engage, read, and adopt. Become comfortable with being uncomfortable.
- **Forgeting hierarchy.** Ask questions, share knowledge. Learn from others.

- **Thinking beyond reality.** Use your imagination without limits – lots of other people will rein you back in.
- **Hanging on to your values.** Remember what is important and set boundaries. Then, act accordingly.

Charlie Feld, who works with global corporations to develop next-generation leaders, observes that "the savvier CEO wants someone on the board who can connect appropriately with management on technology-related issues and make recommendations."[5] Companies making transformational investments need to prioritize adding a director with digital competence.

Regardless of your investment priorities right now, your strategy will evolve over time. To stand the test of time, recruitment of a digital director needs to consider the candidates' skills and experience, and a cultural alignment both with the existing board members and with the direction that the board wants to go.

Starting with skills, if you are recruiting a digital director, don't be swayed by a specific set of technology skills. You may think that block chain or ERP is your next top priority, but the candidate you chose for that specific skill may not be the person to help you anticipate the future. A board candidate chosen for a specific set of technology skills may, through enthusiasm and knowledge, drive a strategic decision toward the skill set that they uniquely bring. Instead, look for a board-capable digital leader with demonstrated, broadly based skills. As with any other director you would recruit, the most important attribute for a digital director is the ability to think about the business rather than the technology. A capable digital director will have the intellectual curiosity to always learn more.

Figure 9.4, Smart Questions for Board Rrecruiting, can augment your nominating committee's usual question set to help you assess more digitally oriented candidates.

In addition to recruiting a technologist with business experience, a critically important attribute to screen for is alignment on culture. Nowhere is the research on cultural alignment more powerful than when you are investing in transformation. Figure 9.5 provides a framework for alignment of cultural considerations, framed in the context of the digital maturity model discussed in Chapter 6.

Look at the attributes that align with your desired digital maturity. If those cultural attributes are not what you would consider to be the primary character of your board, consider whether or to what extent it is in the interest of your board to make a shift.

Make culture an overt qualification. If your strategic direction requires a different perspective, consider asking your nominating committee to bring alternatives including candidates who can balance alignment with the board and alignment with your strategy. That does not mean you should nominate a candidate who is culturally opposed to the current make-up of the board, but do consider moving away from the

Category	Search Committee Question	What to look for	What to avoid
General/ qualifying questions	What are your thoughts about the opportunities/issues in our industry sector?	They have done research–data, facts, examples	Generalized responses; an absence of evidence that they have specifically done research or considered the industry
	(If not offered) What do you think are the specific opportunities or issues in a technology context?	Responses are understandable (not jargon or acronyms), supported by specifics that show research and thought	Techno-jargon, unintelligible thoughts, long-winded or complex answers; Strong positions on "the answer," rather than an open and receptive dialogue with fact-based contribution
	Tell us about any roles (Board or otherwise) that uniquely equip you to add value as a member of the Board when we are dealing with those issues		
Competitive advantage & business performance	Tell us about a particularly challenging strategic situation where you needed to interpret and contribute {if specific topics of interest, insert them into this question–e.g. Big data/ analytics, emerging technology, globalization . . . }	Outcome focused–what was different; specific content may be less important than that you understand the answer; minimal acronyms, and any used are explained; focus on meaningful/measured business value; responses are strategic	Response took more than a few minutes; unintel-ligible; focused on the technology rather than the strategy or business outcome

Figure 9.4 Smart Questions for Board Recruiting

Category	Search Committee Question	What to look for	What to avoid
	Tell us about a situation that you impacted positively, where there was operational risk or operatain leverage was required	Content is relevant, and should resonate with the kind of issues you see; important than that you understand the answer; focus on meaningful/measured business value	Response took more than a few minutes; unintelligible; focused on the technology rather than the business outcome
Risk and Compliance	Tell us about the best risk management process you have worked with, and give us an example of a situation where that process really added value	Look for actual experience with a relatively structured or rigorous process. Risk management is at the core of every Board's governance obligation, so take the opportunity to get more than ject the technology skill. A good candidate will also bring experience in this space, so look for that.	Discussions that focus just on cybersecurity or technical issues, without some alignment to the broader enterprise risk elements of the situation
Achieve Investment Returns and Demonstrate Value (Governance)	Tell us about the most challenging investment governance situation you have had to manage.	Look for (1) prioritization of where to invest as a theme; (2) measured (business) impact considerations; (3) alignment of technology and business value	Response took more than a few minutes; unintelligible; focused on the technology rather than the strategy or business outcome

Figure 9.4 *(Continued)*

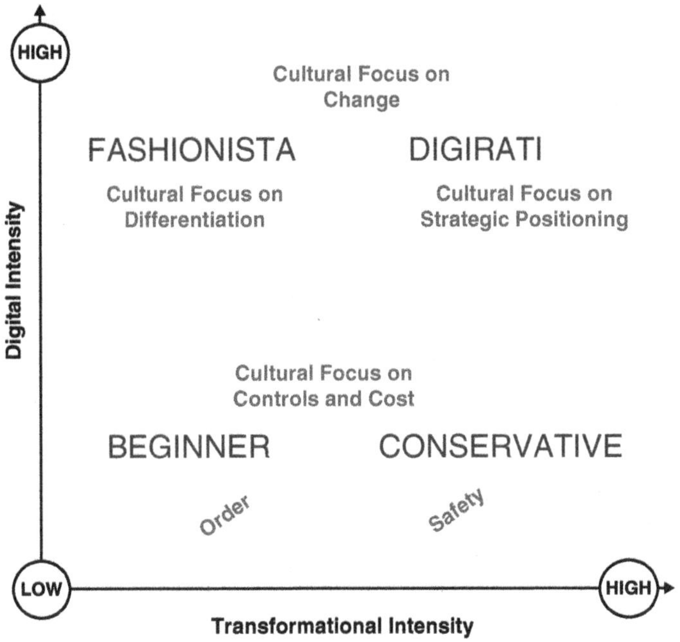
HIGH
Cultural Focus on
Change
FASHIONISTA
DIGIRATI
Cultural Focus on
Differentiation
Cultural Focus on
Strategic Positioning
Digital Intensity
Cultural Focus on
Controls and Cost
BEGINNER
CONSERVATIVE
Order
Safety
LOW
HIGH
Transformational Intensity

Figure 9.5 Cultural Alignment Model

candidate who will primarily reinforce entrenched opinions and expectations.

For example, if your strategic analysis suggests that you need to drive increased digital intensity, your board may need to engage more in more strategic discussions around differentiation. Directors who are predisposed to focus on cost may have a difficult time with the investment decisions you need to make. You may be more successful improving your digital investment acuity if you consider the cultural balance that you need.

If you are looking for a tech-savvy director and you don't yet know what your intended strategy will be, look for some demonstrated success in the relevant segments of the model. There will be clues in the candidate's profile about where on the model they can operate well:

Fashionista (the top left-hand side of the chart) – Evidenced by success on a board or in a company in which specific tactical initiatives have been delivered. Look for the candidate to demonstrate knowledge of the specific business drivers for the investment and what outcomes were measured to support the initiative.

Cultural alignment in this quadrant may indicate the candidate is predisposed to quick wins, so test for long-term and strategic capability.

Digerati (the top right-hand side of the chart) – Demonstrated by success on a board or in a company where measurable strategic transformation has been delivered. Look for the candidate to be able to speak to:

- The value the business realized as a result of investing
- How the impact was realized and measured
- What the specific impacts were in terms of revenue, profit, or operating leverage

Beginner/Conservative (the bottom of the chart) – Cultural alignment would come from experience in a regulated environment, with responsibility for audit or compliance.

When considering longer-term flexibility to move up the model, test whether the candidate can speak to success in an environment that is not rules-based.

Conservative/Digerati (the right-hand side of the chart) – Evidenced by successful delivery of measured transformation, whether it is overt cost take-out or improvement of operating leverage. Specifically, assess whether the candidate understands what cost improvements were delivered and how savings were achieved at a P&L level.

If they directed a change but can't demonstrate an understanding of the drivers for the improvements, they may not really understand what it takes to effect a cost-oriented transformation.

Organizational Leadership and Attitudes

The attitudes across the organization, especially those of your leadership team, can either act as multipliers in your transformation, or they can act as detractors. "Just because the group says yes doesn't mean it's going to happen."[6]

Impactful investments need both intent and focus – "just pulling a lever does not help. You have to pull it hard enough to make a difference."[7] Having clarity will help, but a transformational team will face many barriers to success so they need to pull as hard as they can. Any signs of weakness in their support or commitment can undermine both the way the investments are perceived in the organization and the genuineness of commitment to the outcomes.

> At GE, Jack Welch challenged all of the businesses to be #1 or #2 in their respective markets. Rather than focus on how to grow in their market, the response of leadership was to re-define their markets to align with their ability to position as first or second.[8]

Not to say your leadership team will set such a poor example or set out to obscure their lack of commitment to your digital objectives. They may simply suffer from what MIT calls bias-based behavior,[9] which can take four forms:

- **Halo effect** – The team giving itself a pat on the back for 6% profit growth as a result of digital initiatives and cutting cost, when in fact the entire market grew profits by 6%.
- **Anchoring** – The team starts with a specific business forecast, which becomes the starting point for a negotiation, rather that actively engaging in an analysis of what outcomes are possible.
- **Confirmation bias** – The team engages in all the reasons that an investment will work – effectively confirming an inherent bias – rather than genuinely assessing alternatives.
- **Loss aversion** – The team ignores external threats that an investment can mitigate; instead, it studies only the risks of taking on the investment.

The tone at the top is critical for even modest investments. At minimum, ensure that board-level communications and follow-up set the tone to offset potential bias impacts.

Leadership drives attitudes, and attitudes propagate across the organization. Your investment strategy needs to include overt acts of proactive reinforcement. Whether you consider technology an enabler, a strategy, a product, or a service, it must be clearly perceived as a strategic driver of value.

Legacy Technology

One of the biggest detractors for your strategy will be older "legacy" systems. Those limitations manifest in a few ways:

- **Complexity** – Development work over time has resulted in core systems that are complex and not well understood. As a result, it is prohibitive to modernize processes for fear of the impacts on the systems that support them.

Think of your legacy systems as if they are an old house that has been renovated multiple times. Dropped ceilings hide problems. Wiring has been layered on. The fuse box looks like a snake's nest. Duct tape may be involved. Repairs and renovations are fraught with risk.

- **Capability** – Technology of a certain vintage is simply unable to integrate with newer technology and service-based capabilities. Challenges will be a result of your legacy technology's inability to communicate with the newer forms of digital messaging.

Following the renovation scenario, the cable TV wiring is so out of date that you could not switch to a high resolution TV if you wanted to.

- **Integration** – Old-school methods for integrating systems have created complex dependencies. A change in one system or to one integration point can have significant impacts on other systems or integrations.

When they added on the family room, they dug a separate basement. You cannot get from the laundry room in the new basement to the storage room in the old basement without going up the stairs on one side and then back down on the other side.

- **Tools that don't scale** – Enthusiasm for getting new offerings to market may have resulted in systems that are not robust, or infrastructure that is not sustainable.

That discount air conditioner looked like a really good deal, but it is freezing in the kitchen and the rest of the house is still too warm.

- **Sheer order of magnitude** – Volume is generally an issue with legacy data, rather than legacy systems. Large organizations will often spend far too much of their IT budget maintaining data that is years, even decades, old. Even worse, when those companies invest in more strategic projects like moving data to the cloud, they invest in both the effort and the ongoing expense to move all the data that they have without assessing how old it is, and how old is relevant.

Do you really need to build shelving for those boxes of bank statements and cheques from the 1970s?

If you have legacy issues, they have evolved over time. Fear of changing your legacy environment is legitimate, but you cannot let that hold you back. Every year you will get further behind. If you have any of these legacy environment issues, the first step in your digital strategy probably needs to be to neutralize your legacy exposures.

If your team suggests that your legacy environment is holding you back, your CIO should deliver a strategy to address the problem. (If they cannot, you may have the wrong CIO.)

Remediation or replacement of legacy systems is an investment decision in and of itself. As part of defining your digital investments, look for your CIO to be fact-based and proactive about where investments should be diverted to more strategic work. If your legacy environment cannot be part of the solution, it is probably part of the problem.

Uncoupling legacy system issues can be an overwhelming investment for some organizations, so here are some discussion points to help you test the boundaries. There are five legacy system issues that drive a legitimate need for remediation:

1. Complexity of core (legacy) systems
2. Inability to integrate
3. Complex dependencies
4. Lack of infrastructure and tools
5. Legacy data

Proposals brought to the board should specifically speak to the following mitigation strategies.

Legacy System Remediation Strategies

Limitation	Mitigation strategies
Complex core systems	Options to replace your core systems should be considered on a spectrum. Full replacement of your legacy system is at one extreme. The ideal strategy would speak to a packaged solution or an SaaS approach, to deliver industry best-practice in a sustainable model. If this is your plan, the investment will be significant. This is the Loblaw scenario – you probably want to have digital competence on your board to participate in oversight. At the other end of the spectrum your legacy system may be considered so large and complex that a strategic replacement is not viable. In that instance, oversight is based on an as-is and to-be architecture. The focus would be iterative, with progressive steps to uncouple the processes and functions: • Start by uncoupling those functions and processes that are most aligned with your digital strategy. If you want to integrate your supply chain processes with mobile technology and scanners to enable M2M, start by uncoupling the supply chain elements of the legacy systems. • Don't lose sight of the cost of operating your legacy environment; keep an eye on the inflection point where you should be seeing investment proposals to decommission the legacy system.

Limitation	Mitigation strategies
Inability to integrate	Look to your enterprise architect to develop a plan for an integration layer that translates between the old systems and the new channels for access (such an architecture is known as a middle-tier—an architectural translation layer that allows the legacy system or data database to be interpreted out to a flexible array of channels for access): • Look for a short-term investment in a transitional state. Then move proactively to get your complex legacy systems replaced. • Consider ways to robustly provide the data from the legacy system, without having to actually replace the systems. This may imply some level of maintenance of the legacy environment, so understand how much you are just pushing out the problem.
Complex dependencies	If your complexity is in both the systems and the integrations, you will need to invest in a combination of the mitigation strategies in the preceding two sections.
Lack of infrastructure and tools capability	This is the most frustrating kind of investment to have to make. It is spending money to remediate because someone made short-term investment decisions in your past. Now you have to invest just to maintain the status quo:

(*continued*)

Limitation	Mitigation strategies
	• Assess the strategic positioning of whatever is out of date or inadequate. If it is not on your roadmap for the future, maybe it can be decommissioned instead of being remediated • See if SaaS or other modern delivery strategies provide a better option than simply fixing a past mistake. • If the business leaders who made those trade-offs are still with the organization, address the underlying attitude issues (hint: it is unlikely that your CIO drove these short-term decisions).
Legacy data	As part of looking at how you spend your IT budget, you should know how much of your money is maintaining historical data, and how old that data is: • Assess how old is relevant. Consider regulatory requirements as well as practical or historical interest in drawing comparisons or analysis. • Look at retention policies. There is a difference between client business records and sales or analytic data. Look at whether some shorter retention policies are appropriate. • Where you are investing in new systems or methods of data management, always look for the associated decommissioning plans for the legacy components.

Your CIO needs to be your most important ally in your legacy remediation journey. Getting to spending 25% of your digital investment on transformation may not be attainable without it. Take the time to understand your 'to-be' plan.

Culture of Innovation

Think of a culture of innovation as what raises your digital strategy to an art rather than a science. Most technology decisions have multiple options, so seeing investments in technology as absolute may leave opportunities on the table. The sheer magnitude of the options, combined with the pace of change, means that oversight is often making your best decision in the moment and then managing the outcomes. Your team needs to have a bias for innovation to make the continual adjustments it takes to be successful.

Consider the example of Kodak. If its culture had been one of innovation, the company might have found products or partnerships that would let them stay relevant in the transformative period of cell-phones as cameras. Unfortunately for them, they did not.

Digital transformation needs to be more than a footnote in your board documents. It is cultural and demands clarity of strategic insight. Make sure that innovation translates to an approved digital strategy. Take the time to post-mortem unsuccessful investments. Expect regular conversations, not just updates.

Organizational (Political) Challenges

To think through the multiplier and detractor effects of internal politics, you need to pause and consider the stakeholders. Research shows that "internal politics, including fear of losing power in the organization, will impede adoption"[10] of technology strategies.

At the heart of successfully addressing political challenges is the fact those different digital investments will have different stakeholders. Stakeholder issues can disrupt transformation. If one initiative is the target of multiple barriers (otherwise known as excuses to not engage), the risk of failure is high.

Where stakeholders are clearly identified and taking ownership, organizational politics will be a multiplier. Where stakeholders see some outcomes as counter to their objectives or interests, organizational politics will be a detractor. Given the importance of your digital strategy and the relative size of transformational investments, it is critical to understand and be overt in considering who is invested in what strategy and the relationships between stakeholders.[11]

There are (at least) three culture dynamics to consider:

1. **The predictable power struggles.** Because technology is generally a shared resource, it is a magnet for disruptive behavior and power struggles:

- Larger departments often believe that they are entitled to the larger share of the investment, regardless of strategic alignment.
- Revenue-generating departments will feel that they are entitled to dictate the priorities, regardless of the opportunity for operating leverage or the fact that the delivery side of the business is a bottleneck for growth.
- Operating units will endeavor to sway priority by driving messages of urgency, increased headcount, and risk as priorities in the funding dynamic.

Look for your organization to have, and adhere to, a prioritization methodology for all IT investment. Then, when you do have a digital strategy defined and are ready to adjust investments, that method will raise the priority of the right initiatives. Your company needs to operationalize the process to make sure that the tough decisions get acted on.

2. **The mind-altering power of luck.** The book *Thinking in Bets* observes that there is a gap between the bias we apply toward our own success and how we view the success of others.[12] It notes that we tend to identify our own success as a result of skillful planning and execution, and our failure is attributed to bad luck. The success of others is attributed to luck, and their failure is attributed to a lack of planning or skill.

   Be mindful of situations in which the success of others is diminished to enable vested strategic blocks.

3. **The power of outcomes.** By focusing on the measurable outcomes of each strategic investment, the board can rise above the politics and keep the organization focused. If outcome-based progress reports are expected and discussed at the board level, they carry more weight, and there is a clear message for everyone to be working to deliver on the outcomes committed.

   Transformational investments reflect on the board. As such, the board should talk to the CEO about how they expect political behavior to be addressed.

Measurements and Incentives

If you have ever worked in an incentive-based job, or led an incentive-based team, you know that rewarding success will drive self-motivation and initiative. The same is true if you put incentives on transformation. More than 60% of companies who fit into the Digital Beginner quadrant on transformational maturity do not align incentives with transformation. In contrast, 68% of companies in the Digirati quadrant do align incentives with strategic results.[13]

If you have aggressive targets that demand alignment and engagement, incentives can underscore the commitment of the organization. If an organization has committed funding for a critical technology investment, and the only person who has a related incentive is the CIO, that initiative starts out at a disadvantage. To avoid gamesmanship, all stakeholders need to be incentivized toward the same defined outcomes.

There are three unique variables when aligning incentives with transformational investments:

1. **Make it clear when a project is experimental, like a pilot.** Some things will not work technically, but you do not know until you try. Putting an incentive on making it work will not change the outcome. If an investment is to test an outcome or prove that something works, align incentives with the creativity, positioning for next steps and learning.
2. **Make it safe to fail.** Even if an investment has a good chance of being successful, there may be an element of risk due to things that are outside the control of the team. The team is better to declare the failure as soon as they are certain, but they may not do so if they will be penalized.
3. **Apply an incentive strategy to the whole team.** Some participants in a team will be delivering the shiny objects and some will be doing the heads-down work to support the program. They are all making a contribution. Do not give all the glory to the shiny-objects part of the effort.

Consider the example of an FBI unit going after a gang that intends to rob one of three banks. They send a team to stake out each bank, but only one team will capture the robbers. Should they be the only team to get recognized?[14]

Understand what you are expecting to be different, and overtly measure and incent the people who will make that change successful (including the CEO).

Skills

It is critical that skills are not an afterthought. Boards investing in transformational strategies should look beyond the traditional compensation committees and consider talent and rewards committees, or people committees.

Once the board has adopted a digital strategy, and the CEO has turned that strategy into actionable investments, it is critical to know who the key people are for execution. That's not to say that your company should be held to ransom by anyone because they have critical skills. Instead, your company should avoid a skills-crisis by aligning your digital and people strategies proactively. A successful skills strategy will focus on keeping an engaged and motivated team, rather than having to recruit, retrain, or save employees because of critical skills gaps.

Your digital strategy should be clear about the skills-based assumptions and commitments that need to be made. Consider, for example, a decision to pilot block chain. That project will force your company to find skills you do not have. Even if you turn to an outside expert, how will your CIO know whether they were successful? A decision to proceed beyond the pilot will create a dependence on having those skills, so your pilot also needs to lay the foundation to find or build the capability. Research suggests that skills will be the top obstacle for the adoption of emerging technologies like block chain and Internet of Things.[15]

Take the time to ask questions about your transformation skill strategies, including IT skills. If you are investing in strategic digital capabilities you may want to also invest in sustainable team engagement. There are three ways to build stickiness:

First, align resourcing strategies with long-term needs – Access to highly skilled contractors has changed the basic rules of work for most IT people. The industry demands that people keep up core skills, but many companies hire contractors for the high value, skilled work as an alternative to supporting the cost of training. As a result, employees see little value in being committed long term, and they believe that they need to move companies to get experience.

If you care about having a team you can count on, make sure that your IT people get the training they need to stay current and improve their skills. There is a place for using external experts, but don't let critical internal people be repeatedly overshadowed or left behind by outside experts.

Outsourcing is also a frequently raised but complex resourcing option. Before you decide that it is a viable strategy, be fact-based on what outsourcing means and where it is (and is not) helpful. The notes in Figure 9.6 will help you be fact-based about the outsourcing option.

Second, acknowledge commitment – The commitment of highly skilled staff members, particularly those who stick with you through long hours and challenging work, is worthy of acknowledgement. For most IT people, that doesn't mean getting them on the

What it is – going to an outside service provider to take over a specific part of your IT function with full responsibility for how it goes and if it works.

Why you would outsource:

- Highly expert activities are in the hands of the experts. For example, using a "managed service" like cloud-based Salesforce CRM can save your staff from having to become experts in setting up and managing a salesforce environment. They can have service levels and manage to ensure that they get the delivery, support and auditability that they need.
- Specific tasks or deliverable get done without distraction for the team. This only works if and when the work can truly be done independent of the internal or nuanced business requirements. if an internal person has to work closely with the outsourced team to get the work done, it is kind of like the old consultant joke – they are borrowing your watch to tell you the time.
- The outsourced activity is truly end-of-life and adds no long-term business value, like archiving legacy data, so outsourcing lets you clearly contain the time and money that will be spent.
- Cost savings. Be cautious with this benefit. Outsourcers who promise annual savings do so by taking annual reductions in the staff and effort that they put into your support. You can only take so many 10% reductions before you are not getting much support, and there is a significant cost and disruption to outsource and then bring activities back in house when it doesn't meet your needs.
- Capitalization. Outsourcing makes it easier to identify the cost to build an asset, which makes it easier to put a box around development costs that you would capitalize, but that should be a secondary benefit. Clear rules and time reporting can also provide auditable evidence to support calling development CAPEX. The visual below shows if and when outsourcing of development is useful.

Specifications are clear
Outsource
Keep Control
Nothing is business unique

It may be helpful to outsource for clearly defined processes and activities that do not have business nuance. If a requirement is really well understood, and can be measured and managed with sevice levels or proof that it works, a process or task can potentially be outsourced. It is not helpful to outsource just because the business wants more from the IT team. If the outsourcing is a distraction, they may be exacerbating whatever problem they have with resources. Your CIO should have an opinion, and be the gate, on any notion of outsourcing.

Figure 9.6 A Side Note on Outsourcing

stage and giving them awards – they really do believe that they are just doing their job. But a comment in the elevator that actually shows that an executive realizes what they contributed a few days off after a particularly challenging project, or a personal note of acknowledgement, will go a long way with this generally humble and introverted group.

Finally, reward behavior – Savvy CIOs will take a solid developer with the right values over a whiz kid with a big ego any day. No part of the business is more dependent on teamwork than IT, so listening and engagement skills are critical. Your CIO is often the one expected to take the high road and model the right behavior; so a proactive people strategy needs to reward behavior as much as outcomes.

Skills will be a critical contributor to your strategic success, so take the time to show your interest.

* * *

As a director, your role is to be "nose in, fingers out." That implies a balance in considering the multipliers and detractors because they are often tightly coupled with operational execution and management. Awareness will help you know *when* to be nose in. The smart questions provided in Figure 9.7 will help you know *how* to be nose in when you need to.

As a final guide on the topic of oversight, the book *Strategy Beyond the Hockey Stick* offers five principles for general investment success. Those same five rules work well to have the right multipliers for your technology investment[16]:

1. **Be programmatic.** Some things you try will not work out, so you need a steady pipeline of aligned initiatives

Board Skill

- Do we have the skills to effectively challenge management decisions on technology investments?
- Do we understand our investments and risks enough to be accountable?
- What skills do we need to improve and how should we do that?

Core Detractors

- What attitudes, technology, culture, politics, and skills may be holding us back ?
- What is our legacy technology and data situation, and what are our opinions on the need to replace or remediate?
- What are the organizational strengths in technology-based investment and transformation?
- What are the organizational weaknesses in technology-based investment and transformation?
- How would we characterize our leaders' abilities to engage in and foster our strategic initiatives?
- Have we had an independent assessment of values, culture and organizational alignment?
- What are our critical skill areas? How are we building our strength, capacity, and retention for those skills?
- Looking at actually delivering change (not just having ideas), who are our strongest innovation leaders?

Measures & Incentives

- What specific transformation outcomes or differences are we expecting this year? How will we measure success?
- What specific transformation outcomes or differences are we planning for next year? What do we expect to be different by the end of next year?
- Do we have leadership incentives aligned with those strategic and transformation initiatives?

Figure 9.7 Smart Questions – Oversight

that will move you toward your desired state. That pipeline can include pilot projects, partnerships with suppliers, new products, or acquisitions for capability or market share – whatever fits with your strategy. But do not pick one thing, and then sit back. Your digital investment roadmap should be dynamic and forward-looking, to make the board and CEO's commitment clear to the organization and the investors.

2. **Dynamic reallocation of resources.** Do not do the peanut-butter-spread thing. A proactive focus on leadership, legacy systems, and innovation demands that

you regularly push some limits and adjust your investments to fund what is most important.

3. **Strong capital investment.** To beat the odds, the McKinsey research suggests that your ratio of *capital spending to sales needs to be in the top 20% in your industry.*

4. **Strength of productivity program.** Strategic digital investment should drive productivity improvements, so be sure that operating leverage comes through in downstream business plans.

5. **Improvements in differentiation.** Digital investments can be key differentiators, in small measures like customer engagement and in large measures like market share. Don't just look for the financial differentiation. While you are investing in strategic transformation, expect to see differentiation in culture and your ability to attract and retain talent. Consider all the ways that you want the organization to stand out, and look for ways to make your digital investments support those objectives.

Notes

1. M. Fitzgerald, N. Kruschwitz, D. Bonnet, and M. Welch, "Embracing Digital Technology: A New Strategic Imperative," *MIT Sloan Management Review* (October 7, 2013).

2. C. Stephenson and N. Olson, "Why CIOs Make Great Board Directors," *Harvard Business Review* (December 20, 2017).

3. M. Eyre, "Leading in a Digital World," *Forbes* (February 14, 2017).

4. Ibid.

5. C. Stephenson and N. Olson, "Why CIOs Make Great Board Directors," *Harvard Business Review* (December 20, 2017).

6. C. Bradley, M. Hirt, and S. Smit, *Strategy Beyond the Hockey Stick* (Hoboken, NJ: John Wiley & Sons, 2017), p. 33.

7. Ibid, p. 168.

8. Ibid, p. 19.

9. M. Fitzgerald, N. Kruschwitz, D. Bonnet, and M. Welch, M. "Embracing Digital Technology: A New Strategic Imperative." *MIT Sloan Management Review* (October 7, 2013).

10. Ibid.

11. B. Groysberg, J. Lee, J. Price, and J. Cheng, "The Leader's Guide to Corporate Culture: How to Manage the Eight Critical Elements of Organizational Life," *Harvard Business Review* (January–February 2018).

12. A. Duke, *Thinking in Bets, Making Smarter Decisions When You Don't Have All the Facts* (New York: Penguin, 2017).

13. Fitzgerald, Kruschwitz, Bonnet, and Welch, "Embracing Digital Technology."

14. Bradley, Hirt, and Smit, *Strategy Beyond the Hockey Stick*, p. 89.

15. C. Bradley, M. Hirt, and S. Smit, "Strategy to Beat the Odds," *McKinsey Quarterly* (February 2018).

16. Ibid.

Chapter 10

Governance

Amazon stands out as the poster child for governance in digital strategy and technology investment. The Amazon board drives value based on three enduring principles:

1. Focus on the customer.
2. Test market opportunities made available by technology.
3. Focus on data driven analysis to improve results.

Amazon started with word matching and search optimization (SEO), building millions of key words for customer search as the foundation for engagement and growth.

Market Summary > Amazon.com, Inc.
NASDAQ: AMZN
1,663.15 USD 0.00 (0.00%)
Jun. 25, 4:00 p.m. EDT · Disclaimer
1 day
5 days
1 month
1 year
5 years
Max
2,000
1,500
1,000
500
0
1998
2002
2006
2010
2014
2018

Source: NASDAQ

Over time, Amazon has led the industry by progressively delivering clear and simple experiences through testing with customers and responding to needs.

Amazon leads the industry in delivering personalization, with relevant recommendations based on a customer's buying behavior.

The frictionless purchase decision that Amazon Prime enables is an impactful example of a mature and proactive digital strategy. Amazon has consistently topped the American Customer Satisfaction Index (ACSI) since 2000, and they are at the top of their sector for revenue per unique visitor.

The power of governance shows in Amazon's share price.

The case of Amazon takeaway ➔ Just because there is technology involved, do not lose sight of the basics. Stay focused on where the facts take you, and do what makes sense.

Figure 10.1 The Case of Amazon

The case of Amazon, in Figure 10.1, demonstrates the power of being focused on both the enhancement and the protection of shareholder value. There are two specific standards of performance:

1. **Fiduciary duty**, which requires the individual director to act with honesty, in good faith, and in the best interest of the company.
2. **Duty of care**, which requires the individual director to engage with care, diligence, and skill, and to make decisions that are prudent and reasonable.

It has historically been enough for a board to rely on experts in areas like technology. With incidents involving systemic breaches of privacy, like Target, and business models that go beyond expected norms, like Facebook, directors are increasingly under pressure to have their own level of technology diligence and skill in order to fulfill the "protect" part of their mandate.

Enhance and protect are the flip sides of the same coin, and directors need to be on top of both.

> *Governance is like steering, Risk Management is like braking.*
>
> Pearl Zhu

Technology governance discussions often focus only on the risk issues, which leave most boards with a blind spot regarding the opportunities. The blind spot is made larger by the traditional approach of governance by exception.

When a board counts on the CEO to know what to bring in for discussion, it is often left out of the digital investment conversation entirely.

Industry experts now suggest "technology governance has become integral to corporate governance because it can impact multiple areas of corporate risk, including reputation and changing requirements for IT disclosure. Incompetence, or even reduced competence, can be very costly in a digital era. This is evidenced by the Target US case, as well as the growing list of iconic brands that have either gone out of business or that have lost significant market share. Many simply did not see digital disruption coming, or worse they lacked the capability to recognise that digital change was relevant to them."[1] Further, "how a company implements and represents its corporate social responsibility and sustainability practices may affect its operations, financial performance, corporate governance, and reputation."[2]

Best practice frameworks identify three broadly based governance competencies as critical:[3]

1. The ability to govern technology for strategic performance and to enhance organization performance.
2. The ability to make quality judgements and decisions in relation to business technology and data use, including technology risk.
3. The ability to oversee technology projects to achieve returns and demonstrate value.

It is insufficient for the board to say that they delegated responsibility to the CEO when major strategic investments fail. It is strategically important that the board have measurable indicators of progress and defined outcomes, and that they regularly monitor the results. Anything less can be seen as a failure of governance.[4]

As an experienced director you understand the fundamentals of governance, but gaps can occur when conversations become 'too' technical. There are things you can do:

- **Engage in more of a dialogue.** By being more authentically engaged in the discussion, you can offer better challenges and you can look for an improved quality of ideas coming to your board. Use the smart questions offered in each of the chapters. Then, actively listen to the answers and ask more questions until you understand what you need to know.
- **Give time and priority to your doubts.** You are a director because you have proven that your instincts are well developed. If you do not understand the topic, you are right to be skeptical. You do not have to buy everything the CIO or anyone else is selling. Use the smart questions that follow to either get past your doubts or to just say no.
- **Do not get distracted by technical terms.** If you are reading this book, you are ready to engage enough to understand the decisions that you are being asked to make. If your CIO cannot help you understand what you need to know, then you may have the wrong CIO.
- **Do not tolerate "eyes glazed over" by your peers on the board.** If other directors seem disengaged, look for

your leadership team to bring the conversation up to a level that is engaging. Find an analogy that will resonate on the issues and the decisions to be made. Use examples. Discuss it privately if need be; only another director can call out this behavior for the problem that it is.

- **Look for independent views.** Use methods like the earlier 'how to avoid group think' practices, to have less biased, better calibrated decisions.
- **Avoid "agreement by exhaustion".** Dean Acheson, Secretary of State under Truman, coined that phrase to describe the situation in which experts are unrelenting. Decisions get ratified because decision makers want the discussion to stop.
- **Lead your team with courage.**
- **Take informed and calculated risks.**
- **Vigorously commit**. Understand what it will take to get the outcome you need.

The bottom line in technology governance is to just get started; it will get easier. Challenge yourself to get better. See the Smart Questions shown in Figure 10.2.

There are many ways to center a business. You can be competitor focused, you can be product focused, you can be technology focused, you can be business model focused, and there are more. But in my view, obsessive customer focus is by far the most important. Even when they don't yet know it, customers want something better, and your desire to delight customers will drive you to invent on their behalf.

Jeff Bezos

- Have we challenged management to include board review and approval in our technology strategy? Do we receive updates on how that strategy is progressing?
- What decisions are we delegating that we should be more involved in?
- Does technology make it possible for us to do something new or different?
- Are we effectively discussing the opportunities to enable value creation?
- What changes are we making that could impact our policies?
- Are we truly accountable for our decisions relating to IT?
- How much are we or our leadership team expecting outside experts to be accountable for technology decisions?
- Are the decisions we delegate appropriate? What is the risk?
- Do we provide effective oversight of risk in relation to digital investments?

Figure 10.2 Smart Questions – Governance

Notes

1. E. Valentine, "Enterprise Technology Governance: New Information and Technology Core Competencies for Boards of Directors, Professional Doctorate thesis, Queensland University of Technology, 2016, p. 235.
2. Ibid, p. 234.
3. Ibid, p. 198.
4. "Why Single Out Technology Governance for Board Attention?" *Enterprise Governance Blog* (February 16, 2014).

BUZZWORDS, ACRONYMS, AND LEGITIMATE TERMINOLOGY

AASB	Audit and Assurance Standards Board (see also ISAE)
Agile (Agility)	A method of project management, used especially for software development, that is characterized by the division of tasks into short phases of work and frequent reassessment and adaptation of plans
Android phone	A *smartphone* operating system (OS) developed by Google
API	Application programming interface (a set of subroutine definitions, protocols, and tools for building application software; commonly makes it easier to develop a computer program by providing all the building blocks, which are then put together by the programmer)
Application software	A program (*application* or app for short) designed to perform a group of coordinated functions, tasks, or activities for the benefit of the user

Artificial intelligence (AI)	Intelligence demonstrated by machines, in contrast to the natural intelligence (NI) displayed by humans and other animals; commonly defined as any device that perceives its environment and takes actions; colloquially when a machine mimics cognitive functions that humans associate with other human minds, such as learning and problem solving
Augmented reality	A direct or indirect view of a physical, real-world environment whose elements are augmented by computer-generated perceptual information; commonly used across multiple sensory modalities, including visual, auditory, haptic, somatosensory, and olfactory
Bar code	An optical, machine readable, representation of data, usually describing something about the object that carries the barcode or identifying the object; traditional barcodes represent data by varying the widths and spacing of parallel lines; more recently, bar codes include two-dimensional geometric patterns with unique identifying capability
BCI	Brain–computer interface (using human neural activity, information is encoded and used to stimulate the brain)
Big Data	Extremely large data sets that may be analyzed computationally to reveal patterns, trends, and associations, especially relating to human behavior and interactions

Black swan events	An event or occurrence that deviates beyond what is normally expected of a situation and is extremely difficult to predict; black swan events commonly considered random and unexpected
Block chain	A distributed record keeping concept, with unique digital attributes that can manage unique access and keep data immutable
CCSS	Canada's Cyber Security Strategy
CFAA	Computer Fraud and Abuse Act (US legislation that prohibits accessing a computer without authorization, or in excess of authorization)
CCIRC	Canadian Cyber Incident Response Centre
CISA	Cyber Information Sharing Act (US)
Closed architecture	A system whose technical specifications are not made public; restricts third parties from building products that interface with or add enhancements; contrasts with open architecture
Cloud computing	An information technology (IT) paradigm that enables ubiquitous access to shared; pools of configurable system resources and higher-level services that can be rapidly provisioned with minimal management effort, often over the Internet; commonly recognized as computing that relies on sharing of resources to achieve coherence and economies of scale, similar to a public utility

Cognitive computing Simulation of human thought processes in a computerized model; self-learning systems that use data mining, pattern recognition, and natural language processing to mimic the way the human brain works

Configurable A method of setting parameters for a computer system to manage input permitting the administrator to select from a defined set of parameters or options, rather than developing custom software code to define format or options. As an example, most enterprise software permits selection of configurable options available for format of names; where the options for titles can be extensive, the administrator can define a more manageable list with the simple options being Mr., Mrs., or Miss. A more comprehensive set of options might include Dr. and Ms. – that would be a configurable decision.

COTS Common Off The Shelf, a phrase used to identify industry-standard software being in use rather than customized or internally developed systems software

CRM Customer relationship management, an approach to manage a company's interaction with current and potential customers; commonly uses data analysis about customers' history to improve business relationships; software that provides foundational source of data for customer analytics, modeling, and retention; commonly seen as an enabler for sales growth

Cryptocurrency	A digital or virtual currency that uses cryptography for security; considered to be difficult to counterfeit because of this security feature; because it is not issued by any central authority, commonly considered the currency of choice among cyber-criminals (see https://coinmarketcap.com/ for more information)
Customer centricity	A way of doing business with your customer in a way that provides a positive customer experience before and after the sale in order to drive repeat business, customer loyalty, and profits.
Customer lifecycle	Describes the progression of steps a customer goes through when considering, purchasing, using, and maintaining loyalty to a product or service
Data Definition Specification	*(DDS) A* guideline to ensure comprehensive and consistent data definitions; commonly defined at an enterprise level to prevent duplication and ensure consistency
Data dictionary	A set of information describing the contents, format, and structure of a database and the relationship between its elements; commonly used to control access to and manipulation of the database
Data mining	The practice of examining large databases in order to generate new information
Data scrubbing	Also called data cleansing; the process of amending or removing data in a database that is incorrect, incomplete, improperly formatted, or duplicated

Data warehouse	A large store of data accumulated from a wide range of sources within a company and used to guide management decisions
DDoS	Distributed denial of service (occurs when multiple systems flood the bandwidth of a targeted system, causing the volume to exceed the available capacity)
Digital tag	A keyword or term assigned to a piece of information (such as an Internet bookmark, digital image, database record, or computer file) used to describe an item and allow it to be found again by browsing or searching
DNS	Domain Name System-hierarchical decentralized naming system for computers, services, or other resources connected to the Internet or a private network; associates various information with assigned names (domain names)
DoS	Denial of service (involving one computer and one Internet connection)
DSS	Data Security Standard
DT	Digital Technology
EA	Enterprise Architecture
e-business	Any kind of business or commercial transaction that includes sharing information across the Internet; commonly referred to as e-commerce
Encryption key	A random string of bits created explicitly for scrambling and unscrambling data; encryption keys are designed with algorithms intended to ensure that every key is unpredictable and unique; the longer the key built in this manner, the harder it is to crack the encryption code

End-to-end	A term used in many business arenas referring to the beginning and end points of a method or service; a theory that embraces the philosophy that eliminating as many middle layers or steps as possible will optimize performance and efficiency in any process; commonly considered to be the definition of using the most efficient and timely approach to manufacture goods or complete a service
Enterprise Application Suite	Systems used to enable collaborative initiatives such as supply chain management (SCM), customer relationship management (CRM), and business intelligence (BI) among business partner organizations through the use of various e-business technologies
Enterprise architecture	The strategic and integrative alignment of technology investment plans with a complete expression of the enterprise; provides a master plan or collaborative force to align goals, vision, strategy, and governance in an executable framework
ERM	Enterprise risk management (the methods and processes used by organizations to manage risks; commonly seen as the framework for risk management, which typically involves identifying particular events or circumstances relevant to the organization's objectives, assessing them in terms of likelihood and magnitude of impact, determining a response strategy, and monitoring progress)

ERP	Enterprise resource planning (a process by which a company manages and integrates the important parts of its business; commonly refers to software or a management information system that integrates areas such as planning, purchasing, inventory, sales, marketing, finance, and human resources)
ETG	Enterprise technology governance (appropriate terminology to address the oversight requirements of a board)
FISMA	Federal Information Security Management Act (US regulation governing government information security practices)
Full stack	Working with systems infrastructure (hardware), OS (operating system), and systems and dependencies for all software.
Gamification	The application of game-design elements and game principles in nongame contexts; commonly used to improve user engagement, organizational productivity, ease of use; commonly thought to improve ability to comprehend digital content
GEIT	Governance of enterprise information technology
Geo-fencing	A virtual perimeter for a real-world geographic area; could be dynamically generated as a boundary around a specific location, or a predefined set of boundaries; commonly used to communicate with a location-aware device to trigger an alert to the device's user as well as the geo-fence operator

Globalization	The process by which businesses or other organizations develop international influence or start operating on an international scale
HCM	Human capital management; the management of skills, qualifications, training levels, and productivity of a workforce.
Insights	Realized patterns based on interpretation of data or observations
Intelligent software	Software that uses artificial intelligence (AI) in the pursuit of defined processes or goals; commonly means the use of software to deliver outcomes without human intervention
Interoperability	Characteristic of a product or system, whose interfaces are completely understood, to work with other products or systems, at present or future, in either implementation or access, without any restrictions
IoT	Internet of Things (broadly describes the cyber universe of mobile and connected devices, including traditional devices, appliances, wearables . . .)
ITG	Information technology governance (outdated term for governance of IT – see ETG)
ISAE	International Standard on Assurance Engagements (foundation for global consistency in audit and compliance requirements – see also AASB)
KEAS	Knowledge, Experience, Attitudes, and Skills

Lighting Up Phones Reference to an event or incident, probably social media in nature, that causes a sudden and dramatic increase in conversations within a specific social network; common phraseology includes "my phone blew up"

LTSCDA Long-Term Sustainable Competitive Differentiated Advantage

Machine to machine Direct communication between devices using any communications channel, including wired and wireless; can include industrial instrumentation, enabling a sensor or meter to communicate data to application software that can use it

MOOC Massive Open Online Courses; a transformational trend in the technology sector with Harvard, MIT, Microsoft, and other top universities and institutions in subjects like computer science, data science, business, and more.

Middle Tier An architectural translation layer that allows the legacy system or data database to be interpreted out to a flexible array of channels for access, including potentially flexible APIs that can interface with different technologies or services; traditionally seen as the system layer that presented the data out to the user, but can represent a more flexible interpretation to enable communication between older technology and newer access channels; commonly provides a high-performance engine to interact with the Internet.

Mobile	A computing device small enough to hold and operate in the hand; commonly includes a touchscreen interface; connects to the Internet and interconnects with other devices via Wi-Fi, Bluetooth, cellular networks, or near field communication (NFC); common capabilities include integrated cameras, media players, telephone capability, video games, and global positioning (GPS) capabilities; may also allow third-party apps for additional specific capabilities
Mobile App	A software application developed specifically for use on small, wireless computing devices, such as smartphones and tablets, rather than on desktop or laptop computers
Multi Cloud	The use of *multiple cloud* computing and storage services in a single heterogeneous architecture; also refers to the distribution of software, applications, and so on across several cloud-hosting environments.
Network Multiplier	Technology investments showing higher value (volume) with adoption increases that are outside the enterprise
NFC	Near field communication (enables two electronic devices to establish communication by bringing them within a defined range)
NIFO	Nose in fingers out (board oversight practice)
NIST	National Institute of Standards and Technology (US)
NLP	Natural language processing

Observations	Raw data; commonly the accumulation over time of recorded results or other information
Omni channel	A multichannel sales approach that provides the customer with an integrated customer experience; specifically, the customer can be shopping online from a desktop or mobile device, or by telephone, or in a brick-and-mortar store, and the experience would be seamless
Open Architecture	A system or application design strategy that is intended to make adding, upgrading, and swapping components easy by effectively permitting user-defined code to plug in to an existing foundation
Open Source (OSS)	Denoting software for which versions of the original source code are made freely available and may be redistributed and modified; a misused and maligned term in a controlled technology context, as there are many systems that started as open source code, but have been moved into a secured and managed environment to comply with industry best-practice for controls (as such, they are fully appropriate)
Operating System	The software that supports the actual computer's basic functions, such as scheduling tasks, executing applications, and controlling peripherals; manages the computer environment; as opposed to business-systems software, which delivers specific business functionality or capability

Optimization	An act, process, or methodology of making something (such as a design, system, or decision) as effective as possible; consider the art rather than the science of delivering a system or process at the highest value intersection between investment and capability; commonly (incorrectly) considered making a system or process fully perfect.
OSFI	Office of the Superintendent of Financial Institutions (an independent agency of the government of Canada)
Pattern Recognition	A form of machine learning that focuses on the recognition of patterns and regularities in data; common applications include image recognition for product scans and facial recognition
PCI DSS	Payment Card Industry – Data Security Standard
Personalization	Social media engagement aimed at resonating deeply with customers so that they feel valued and appreciated
Phishing	The attempt to obtain sensitive information such as usernames, passwords, and credit card details (and money), often for malicious reasons, by disguising as a trustworthy entity in an electronic communication. Spear Phishing is overtly targeted toward an individual, organization, or company using specifically compelling subjects such as invoices, shipments, or missed payments.

PIPEDA	Personal Information Protection and Electronic Documents Act (US)
PIPEDA	Personal Information Protection and Electronic Documents Act (Canada)
POS	Point of sale
Predictive Analytics	Predictive modeling, "scoring" data with predictive models, and forecasting; commonly referred to as descriptive modeling and decision modeling or optimization
Rapid Applications Development	(RAD) A suite of software development methodology techniques used to expedite software application development; commonly uses predefined prototyping techniques and tools to produce software applications
RFID	Radio-frequency identification—use of electromagnetic fields to automatically identify and track tags attached to objects
Robotics	Use of computer-controlled robots to perform otherwise manual tasks; commonly used in manufacturing and assembly; increasingly common term used to describe the application of any technology to replace manual, labor-intensive work, including pattern recognition for electronic document review and verification
Root Privileges	The user name or account that by default has access to all commands and files on a Linux or other Unix-like operating system; also referred to as the superuser; required for system environment management but current industry tools enable highly effective restriction and management of use.

SaaS	Software as a Service (a software licensing and delivery model in which software is licensed on a subscription basis and is centrally hosted)
SDLC	Systems development life cycle— a conceptual model used in project management that describes the stages involved in an information system development project, from an initial feasibility study through maintenance of the completed application; often interpreted as best-practice methodology for the alignment and delivery of large system investments.
Sensors	A device, module, or subsystem whose purpose is to detect events or changes in its environment and send the information to other electronics, frequently a computer processor; always used with other electronics, whether as simple as a light or as complex as a computer; common applications include touch sensitivity, pressure measurement, position, temperature, and acceleration
Smartphone	A mobile phone that performs many of the functions of a computer, typically having a touchscreen interface, Internet access, and an operating system capable of running downloaded applications
SMAC	Social, Mobile, Analytics, and Cloud
SMART	Strategy-Matching, Assessable, Relevant, and Technology-Related (competency)

Social media	Computer technologies that facilitate the creation and sharing of information, ideas, career interests, and other forms of expression via virtual networks communities and networks
Social Media Engagement	Methods to understand the behavior of social media marketing-based audiences using definitions of personas (individuals, consumers, and influencers); commonly references relevant attributes of the persona and the measurement framework that might be applied to those personas; applied to marketing functions of strategy, tactics, metrics, and ROI; transformational use in an integrated framework to define how social media marketing activities can be planned, executed, measured, and improved
Social Networks	Digital structures made up of individuals or organizations with digital ties based on other social interactions; commonly provides capability for analyzing and explaining the structure of whole social entities; used to identify local and global patterns, locate influential entities, and examine network dynamics
Software	A program or group of programs designed for end users; commonly divided into two classes: system software—meaning the operating system that runs the computer—and application software, which is purpose specific to support business processes

Software Intelligence	Software designed to analyze source code to better understand Information Technology environments; applies AI (intelligent software) tools and techniques to the mining of data into meaningful and useful information about the technology or system environment
Stakeholder Theory	A theory of organizational management and business ethics that addresses morals and values in managing an organization; originally detailed by Ian Mitroff in 1983
TLA	Three-letter acronym
TSR	Talent, strategy, and risk
Use Cases	A list of actions or event steps typically defining the interactions between a role or function and a system, to achieve a defined goal; commonly shown as the mapping between a type of user or role through specific process steps to deliver a specific outcome
Voice Assistants	Also known as virtual assistants; accessible via multiple methods, such as Google Assistant via chat on the Google Allo app and via voice on Google Home smart speakers; use natural language processing (NLP) to match user text or voice input to executable commands
VR	Virtual reality (a computer-generated scenario that simulates a realistic experience; an immersive environment that can be similar to the real world in order to create a lifelike experience grounded in reality or sci-fi (see also *Augmented reality systems*)

VRIO	Value, Rarity, Imitability, Organization
Wearable Devices	Smart electronic devices (electronic device with micro-controllers) that can be worn on the body as implants or accessories; also referred to as wearables, fashionable technology, wearable devices, tech togs, or fashion electronics; devices that contain effectors enabling objects to exchange data through the Internet without requiring human intervention

RELATED SOURCES AND OTHER READING

Accenture Cyber 2017. www.accenture.com/t20170721T220639Zw/us-en/acnmedia/PDF-57/Accenture-2017-cyber-year-threatscape-report.pdf.

Albizzatti, N. "Unlocking Merger Value, Getting the People Strategy Right." Spencer Stuart (September 2015), https://www.spencerstuart.com/research-and-insight/unlocking-merger-value.

Aron, D., and Waller, G. "Taming the Digital Dragon – the 2014 CIO Agenda," Gartner (2013).

Ashton, K. "That 'Internet of Things' Thing," *RDIF Journal* (22 June 2009). http://www.rfidjournal.com/articles/view?4986.

Baker, G. *20 Questions Directors Should Ask About IT*, 2nd ed., CPA Canada. https://www.cpacanada.ca/en/business-and-accounting-resources/other-general-business-topics/information-management-and-technology/publications/20-questions-on-information-technology

Barlow, J. *Board Member Interview Questions* (25 April 2016). *BoardEffect.com/blog.* www.boardeffect.com/blog/board-member-interview-questions.

Bart, C., *20 Questions Directors Should Ask About Strategy*, CICA. www.nwoinnovation.ca/upload/documents/20qs_strategyeng.pdf

Barton, D., Carey, C., and Charan, R., "An Agenda for the Talent First CEO," *McKinsey Quarterly* (March 2018). https://www.mckinsey.com/business-functions/organization/our-insights/an-agenda-for-the-talent-first-ceo?cid=other-eml-alt-mkq-mck-oth-1803&hlkid=3f3eafeb312447cebe756e6a35baa2b3&hctky=10314066&hdpid=cd7c202e-ac8b-407c-bb0c-4c2e3f9501ae.

BDO Report Says Wide Scale DDoS Attacks Were up by 91% Last Year (20 February 2018). http://ddosattacks.net/bdo-report-says-wide-scale-ddos-attacks-were-up-by-91-last-year/.

Berruti, F., Ross, E., and Weinberg, A. "The Transformative Power of Automation in Banking," McKinsey & Company (November 2017). https://www.mckinsey.com/industries/financial-services/our-insights/the-transformative-power-of-automation-in-banking.

Betts, A. "The New Era of Personalization: The Hyper-connected Customer Experience." *MarTech Today* (23 January 2018). https://martechtoday.com/new-era-personalization-hyper-connected-customer-experience-209529.

Bhatt, G., Emdad, A., Roberts, N., and Grover, V. *Building and Leveraging Information in Dynamic Environments.* https://dl.acm.org/citation.cfm?id=1891155&preflayout=tabs.

Bloch, M., Brown, B., and Sikes, J. "Elevating Technology on the Boardroom Agenda." McKinsey & Company (October 2012). https://www.mckinsey.com/business-functions/digital-mckinsey/our-insights/elevating-technology-on-the-boardroom-agenda.

Bradley, C., Hirt, M., and Smit, S. *Strategy Beyond the Hockey Stick.* Hoboken, NJ: John Wiley & Sons, 2017.

Bradley, C., M. Hirt, M. & Smit, S. "Strategy to Beat the Odds," *McKinsey Quarterly* (February 2018). https://www.mckinsey.com/business-functions/strategy-and-corporate-finance/our-insights/strategy-to-beat-the-odds?cid=podcast-eml-alt-mkq-mck-oth-1802&hlkid=562b3d1ebdcc48cba2b7608fdef21611&hctky=10314066&hdpid=846ac370-100b-44cb-8c3c-ef4b4b830e15.

Bradt, G. "The Only Three True Interview Questions for Potential Board Directors." *Forbes/Leadership* (12 May 2015). https://www.forbes.com/sites/georgebradt/2015/05/12/the-only-three-true-interview-questions-for-potential-board-directors/#196f7f283b60.

Bruemmer, M., "Survey – Most Companies Ill-prepared for a Global Data Breach." *The Experian Data Breach Resolution Blog* (27 June 2017). http://www.experian.com/blogs/data-breach/2017/06/27/survey-companies-ill-prepared-global-data-breach/.

Burke, S. "Ten Jobs That Didn't Exist Ten Years Ago," Digital Marketing Institute (2016). *https://digitalmarketinginstitute.com/blog/10-jobs-didnt-exist-10-years-ago.*

Calder, A. *Growing Up; Practical Strategies for Sustainable Business Growth.* Multi-Media Publications (2009).

Cameron, A., and Samadmoten, D. "Privacy & Cybersecurity Bulletin." *Fasken KnowledgeHub* (20 April 2018). https://www.fasken.com/en/knowledgehub/2018/04/2018-04-17-cybersecurity-risks-for-directors-and-officers-bulletin#similar.

Chou, T. "It's Time for Boards to Have Technology Committees." *CFO Newsletters* (15 April 2014). http://ww2.cfo.com/technology/2014/04/time-boards-technology-committees/.

"The CIO as the Chief Technology Economist to Successfully Guide IT and Digital Investment Strategies." *HMG Strategy – Research Newsletter* (20 December 2017). http://campaign.r20.constantcontact.com/render?m=1102424019438&ca=588e61ae-8f28-4c26-accd-65d75bd1dedd.

Clayton, J. *SEC Statement on Cybersecurity* (20 September 2017). https://www.sec.gov/news/public-statement/statement-clayton-2017-09-20.

Collins, J., BHAG – Big Hairy Audacious Goal – Built to Last excerpt (coauthored with Jerry I Porras). https://www.jimcollins.com/article_topics/articles/BHAG.html.

Complete Guide to Measuring Social Media ROI, Statusbrew blog. https://blog.statusbrew.com/how-to-track-social-media-metrics-and-social-media-ROI.

Concerns About Risks Confronting Boards, EisnerAmper LLP, 2014. www.eisneramper.com/contentassets/6a7512bfd84247edb9eb32a1b94d7cb0/eisneramper-concerns-risks-survey-2014.pdf.

Dann, C., Le Merle, M., and Pencavel, C. *The Root Causes of Value Destruction: How Strategic Resiliency Can Help*. Booz & Co., 2012. https://static1.squarespace.com/static/5481bc79e4b01c4bf3ceed80/t/54e5009de4b0f2941442ff1a/1424294045993/BoozCo_The-Root-Causes-of-Value-Destruction.pdf

Davenport, T. H. *Big Data at Work: Dispelling the myths, uncovering the opportunities*. Boston: Harvard Business School Press, 2014.

DDoS Ring of Fire: DDoS Attack Map That Maps Likelihood of DDoS Attacks, Radware Security. https://security.radware.com/ddos-threats-attacks/ddos-ring-of-fire/

DeNisco Rayome, A. "*42% of the Most Popular Websites Are Vulnerable to Cyberattacks*." TechRepublic.com (6 February 2018). https://www.techrepublic.com/article/42-of-the-most-popular-websites-are-vulnerable-to-cyberattacks/.

"Digital Business Era: Stretch Your Boundaries." Accenture Technology Vision (2015). www.accenture.com/ca-en/_acnmedia/Accenture/Conversion-Assets/Microsites/Documents11/Accenture-Technology-Vision-2015.pdf.

The Digital Tipping Point: McKinsey Global Survey Results (June 2014). www.mckinsey.com/business-functions/digital-mckinsey/our-insights/the-digital-tipping-point-mckinsey-global-survey-results.

"Digital 20/20: Helping Companies Set the Stage for Their Digital Future." *McKinsey Blog*, 21 March 2018). www.mckinsey.com/about-us/new-at-mckinsey-blog/digital-2020-helping-companies-set-the-stage-for-their-digital-future.

"Digitizing Dairy in China." *McKinsey Quarterly* (2018). www.mckinsey.com/global-themes/china/digitizing-dairy-in-china.

Director Lens, Survey Fall 2017, Institute of Corporate Directors & Environics Research Group (2017).

Duke, A. *Thinking in Bets: Making Smarter Decisions When You Don't Have All the Facts*. Penguin 2017.

Eyre, M. "Leading in a Digital World." *Forbes* (14 February 2017). https://www.forbes.com/sites/ciocentral/2017/02/14/leading-in-a-digital-world/#306a6f705fa9.

"Expanding the CISO Role to Drive Innovation with the CEO and the Board." *HMG Strategy Newsletter* (7 March, 2018).

Fitzgerald, M., Kruschwitz, N., Bonnet, D., and Welch, M. "Embracing Digital Technology: A New Strategic Imperative." *MIT Sloan Management Review* (7 October 2013). https://sloanreview.mit.edu/projects/embracing-digital-technology/.

FY 2018 CIO FISMA Metrics, Version 1.0 (31 October 2017). www.dhs.gov/sites/default/files/publications/FY%202018%20CIO%20FISMA%20Metrics_V1_Final%20508.pdf.

"Gartner-Forbes 2012 Board of Directors Survey Shows IT Is at Top of Investment Priorities, Tied With Sales." Gartner Newsroom (23 July 2012). www.gartner.com/newsroom/id/2088815.

"Gartner Identifies the Top 10 Strategic Technology Trends for 2017." Gartner Symposium/ITxpo 2016. www.gartner.com/newsroom/id/3482617.

"Gartner Survey of Asia/Pacific CEOs Reveals Technology Spending Priorities Do Not Match Expectations of Technology," Gartner Newsroom (11 May, 2017). www.gartner.com/newsroom/id/3711317.

"Gartner Survey Shows 42% of CEOs Have Begun Digital Business Transformation," Gartner Newsroom (24 April 2017). https://www.gartner.com/newsroom/id/3689017.

"Gartner CEO and Senior Business Executive Survey Shows that Growth Dominates Key Business Priorities in 2014," Gartner Newsroom (14 April 2014). www.gartner.com/newsroom/id/2707517.

"GDPR Key Changes," EUGDPR Portal (2018). www.eugdpr.org/key-changes.html.

General Data Protection Regulation, Wikipedia (21 February 2018). https://en.wikipedia.org/wiki/General_Data_Protection_Regulation.

Generating Value from Big Data Analytics, ISACA, 2014. http://f6ce14d4647f05e937f4-4d6abce208e5e17c2085b466b98c2083.r3.cf1.rackcdn.com/generating-value-from-big-data-analytics-pdf-2-w-907.pdf.

"Global Study Reveals Gap between CEO Expectations for Digital Transformation and IT Organization Readiness," Commvault.com (8 November 2017). www.commvault.com/news/2017/november/study-shows-gap-between-expectations-for-digital-transformation-and-it-organization-readiness.

'*Governance by Exception' – Are Current Board Processes Too Slow?* (6 February 2015). www.enterprisegovernance.co/blog/governance-exception-are-current-board-processes-too-slow.

Goud, N. *Cyber Attacks on Businesses Cost Investors £ 42 Billion Loss*. https://www.cybersecurity-insiders.com/cyber-attacks-on-businesses-cost-investors-42-billion-loss/.

Groysberg, B., Lee, J., Price, J., and Cheng, J. "The Leader's Guide to Corporate Culture: How to Manage the Eight Critical Elements of Organizational Life." *Harvard Business Review* (January–February 2018). https://hbr.org/product/the-leaders-guide-to-corporate-culture/R1801B-PDF-ENG.

Guilmain, A., Aylwin, A., and Delwaide, K., "*Expect the Intersection of Privacy and AI in 2018.*" *Fasken KnowledgeHub* (16 April 2018). https://www.fasken.com/en/knowledgehub/2018/01/artificial-intelligence-and-the-protection-of-personal-information-in-canada---the-priority-for-2018.

Hacks and breaches: Taming the Cyber Beast. Institute of Corporate Directors, Director Lens (5 February, 2018). www.icd.ca/resource-centre/news-publications/director-lens/.

Improving Board Governance, McKinsey & Company, 2013. www.mckinsey.com/business-functions/strategy-and-corporate-finance/our-insights/improving-board-governance-mckinsey-global-survey-results.

Information Technology – Governance of IT for the Organization. ISO/IES 38500:2015 (Second Edition 2015-02-15; Licensed Download OP-258143).

Janis, I., *Groupthink*. 2nd ed. Houghton-Mifflin, 1982.

Jdouri, S. "42% of Big Businesses Hit by Cyber Security Attacks." Barclay Simpson (19 May 2017). https://www.barclaysimpson

.com/industrynews/bcc-42pcent-of-big-businesses-hit-by-cyber-security-attacks-801836062.

Jones, J. *An Introduction to Factor Analysis of Information Risk (FAIR), A Framework for Understanding, Analyzing, and Measuring Information Risk.* Risk Management Insight (2015). http://www.riskmanagementinsight.com.

Kaarst-Brown, M., and Kelly, S. *IT Governance and Sarbanes-Oxley, Proceedings of the 38th Hawaii International Conference on System Sciences* – 2005.

Kaplan, S., "Leading Disruptive Innovation," *Ivey Business Journal* (2017). http://www.innovation-point.com/wp-content/uploads/2017/03/Leading-Disruptive-Innovation.pdf.

Kahneman, D., *Thinking, Fast and Slow.* Farrar, Straus and Grioux, 2011.

Landi, H. "Survey: 42% of Companies Have Experienced Ransomware Attacks." Healthcare-informatics.com (22 January 2018). www.healthcare-informatics.com/news-item/cybersecurity/survey-42-percent-companies-have-experienced-ransomware-attacks.

Layson, G. "Nissan Canada Finance Reports Data Breach to 1.3 Million Customers." *Automotive News* (21 December 2017). https://canada.autonews.com/article/20171221/CANADA.

Linask, E. *Social Media Is Responsible Business*, The Free Library (1 January 2012). https://www.thefreelibrary.com/Social+media+is+responsible+business-a0281113511.

Linask, E. *Making Sense of Social Media*, Techzone 360 (30 January 2012). www.techzone360.com/topics/techzone/articles/2012/01/30/261062-making-sense-social-media.htm#.

List of Data Breaches, Wikipedia (16 February 2018). https://en.wikipedia.org/wiki/List_of_data_breaches.

Loop, P., and Cline, J., "Five Questions Boards Should Ask About Data Privacy." *NACD Blog* (15 June 2017). https://blog.nacdonline.org/2017/06/five-questions-data-privacy.

Matta, N., and Ashkenas, R. "Why Good Projects Fail Anyway," *Harvard Business Review* (September 2003). https://hbr.org/2003/09/why-good-projects-fail-anyway.

Mobile Fact Sheet, Pew Research Centre (5 February 2018). www.pewinternet.org/fact-sheet/mobile/.

Moller, S. *Maturity in Digital & Social Media,* Digital Public Affairs (7 October 2015). https://steffenmoller.com/tag/corporate-communications/.

Morello, D. "CEO and Senior Executive Survey 2013: CEOs Look Outside for Their Next CIOs," Gartner (23 March 2013).

"No Rewards for 42% of Cyber Security Professionals." Cyber securityJobSite.com (2 March 2017). www.cybersecurityjobsite .com/article/no-rewards-for-42-percent-of-cyber-security-professionals-report-finds/.

Nagle, T., Redman, T., and Sammon, D. "Only 3% of Companies' Data Meets Basic Quality Standards," *Harvard Business Review* (11 September 2017). https://hbr.org/2017/09/only-3-of-companies-data-meets-basic-quality-standards

Nunes, A., and Ferguson, C. "OSS Risks," *Fasken KnowledgeHub* (13 December 2017). https://www.fasken.com/en/knowledge hub/2017/12/mitigating-cyber-security-risks-arising-from-open-source-software.

"Only 43% of Canadian Companies Could Detect a Sophisticated Cyber-attack," *EY Newsroom* (15 February 2017). www.ey.com/ ca/en/newsroom/news-releases.

O'Reilly, L., and McKinnon, J., "Facebook to Check Groups Behind 'Issue Ads'," *Wall Street Journal* (9 April 2018). https://www .wsj.com/articles/facebook-to-check-groups-behind-issue-ads-1523037600.

Parent, M., "What Do Directors Expect from CIOs?" CIO Canada (29 April 2015). http://ciopeerforum.ciocan.ca/past-events/2015/ sessions/15-april-15/29-what-do-directors-expect-from-cios

Peterson, B. "Companies Will Spend $3.5 Trillion on Tech This Year," *Business Insider* (13 July 2017). http://www.businessinsider.com/ worldwide-it-spending-2017-7.

Porter, M., "Five Competitive Forces That Shape Strategy," *Harvard Business Review* (1 January 2008). https://www.isc.hbs .edu/strategy/business-strategy/Pages/the-five-forces.aspx.

Porter, M. "What Is Strategy," *Harvard Business Review* (November–December 1996).

Ragan, S., "10 Mistakes Companies Make after a Data Breach," *CSO* (13 November 2013). https://www.csoonline.com/article/ 2130834/data-protection/128442-10-mistakes-companies-make-after-a-data-breach.html. Retailer Urban Outfitters. https://www .marketingdive.com/news/how-urban-outfitters-leveraged-location-marketing-for-a-75-conversion-gain/436943/

Roettgers, J. "Facebook Data Backlash Reveals Tech's Biggest Challenge: Trust," *Variety* (27 March 2018). http://variety .com/2018/digital/news/facebook-data-crisis-tech-trust-mark-zuckerberg-1202736903/.

Smith, A., and Anderson, *Social Media Use in 2018*, Pew Research Centre (1 March 2018). www.pewinternet.org/2018/03/01/social-media-use-in-2018/.

Stein, L., Wiley, B., and Kardash, A. "CSA Issues Guidance on Cybersecurity and Social Media Practices for Registered Firms," Osler (26 October 2017).

Stephenson, C., and Olson, N. "Why CIOs Make Great Board Directors," *Harvard Business Review* (20 December 2017). https://hbr.org/2017/03/why-cios-make-great-board-directors.

"Taking the Next Step in a CIO's Career," HMG Strategy (12 March 2018). http://campaign.r20.constantcontact.com/render?m=1102424019438&ca=4aedac13-89c7-4c4f-9cdc-0aa8d00f3c09.

Taleb, N. *Fooled by Randomness*. Random House (2010).

Tamturk, V., "Gap Between CEO Expectations and IT Organization Readiness," cms-connected.com (23 November 2017). http://www.cms-connected.com/News-Archive/November-2017/Digital-Maturity-Gap-Between-CEO-Expectations-and-IT-Organization-Readiness.

Thomas, C., "The Corporate Director's Guide to GDPR," *NACD Blog* (17 August 2017).https://blog.nacdonline.org/2017/08/directors-guide-to-gdpr.

Weldon, D. "How Much Does A Data Breach Cost? Here's Where the Money Goes." *CSO* (24 August 2016). https://www.csoonline.com/article/3110756/data-breach/a-deeper-look-at-business-impact-of-a-cyberattack.html.

Westerman, G., Bonnet, D., and McAfee, A. "The Advantages of Digital Maturity." *MIT Sloan Management Review* (20 November 2012). https://sloanreview.mit.edu/article/the-advantages-of-digital-maturity/.

The Whole Target USA Board Is Sued. http://www.enterprisegovernance.com.au/blog

Whyte, G., and Locke, E. *Make Good Decisions by Effectively Managing the Decision Making Process.* Wiley (11 September 2017).

Valentine, E. "Why and How to Build Director and Senior Executive Information Technology Governance Capability." Enterprise Governance Consulting (May 2016). http://www.enterprisegovernance.co/.

Valentine, E. *Enterprise Technology Governance: New Information and Technology Core Competencies for Boards ofDdirectors,* Professional Doctorate thesis, Queensland University of Technology (2016). http://eprints.qut.edu.au/93089/.

Why Do You Need a CSAE 3416 Canadian SOC Report. http://www.auditwerx.com/csae3416/.

"Why Single Out Technology Governance for Board Attention?" *Enterprise Governance Blog* (16 February 2014). www.enterprisegovernance.com.au/blog/why-single-out-technology-governance-board-attention.

York, A., "6 Social Media Trends That Will Take Over 2018," *Sprout Blog* (6 February 2018). https://sproutsocial.com/insights/social-media-trends/.

Zook, C., and Allen, J. *Profit from the Core: A Return to Growth in Turbulent Times*. Wiley (2010).

INDEX

Page references followed by "*f*" indicate an illustrated figure.